BUILD-IT-YOURSELF HOMESTEAD

Compiled by the editors of Organic Gardening and Farming®

By The Editors of
ORGANIC GARDENING
MAGAZINE
© 1980
Rodale Press, Inc.
Emmaus, PA 18049
Fifth Printing 1983

CONTENTS

INTRODUCTION

If you can't drive a nail straight, and don't know which end of a paint brush to hold, this little book obviously can't teach you how.

But if you are typical of the thousands of people who enjoy ORGANIC GARDENING AND FARMING magazine each month, you're the type who is always looking for a way to make things (especially your homestead) a little better, prettier or easier.

What this book can do is give you some good ideas—ideas that have worked for others just like you—and show you the way they improved their homes and surroundings quickly and inexpensively.

None of these ideas were "dreamed up" by any of our editors. Each homestead project was built by one of our readers, who then contributed it to the pages of ORGANIC GARDENING AND FARMING magazine. None are professional gardeners nor builders. Like you and me, they garden because they love wholesome exercise and wholesome organic food. Like you and me, they are no handier with tools than the average person. In some cases, they confess to have done things the way they did simply because it was the easy way, rather than the "right" way.

So, as you read over the following pages, remember to tell yourself, "If he or she could do it, I can do it."

We include a list of tools—not because they are *needed*, but because they make the job easier, and many readers like to find lists of recommended equipment. But remember that many of the following projects can be done without tools; most of them can be done with tools you already have (a saw and hammer are the only "necessities," and they are inexpensive) and all of them can be done with tools that are usually easily borrowed from friends or relatives.

TOOLS NICE TO HAVE

Saw, crosscut
Hammer
Screwdriver
Pencil
Hand or electric ¼-inch drill
Saber saw
Carpenter's square
Tape measure
Cold chisel
Carpenter's chalk line

BACK SAVERS

Railroad ties are the "building locks" for this stacked strawberry ed built by Barbara Bannister of oyne City, MI.

Ms. Bannister's bed of ties happens) be about 12 feet square, but of ourse yours can be as large or small as ou choose. If you haven't got the use f a chain saw for cutting the ties short hen necessary, use a hand saw with ie coarsest teeth you can find (the ewest teeth per inch).

Remember to fill each tier with soil, ien water it and let the soil settle efore adding the next tier of ties.

A raised garden, built up with walls f broken chunks of cement, is Merle indsey's reply to water shortages, ersistent outbreaks of Johnson grass, nd a hard clay soil that dents ickaxes.

After experimenting with boxes :hey rotted out), he switched to scrap ieces of broken cement, free for the auling. But first he laid out black lastic sheeting over a 25-by-5-foot rea to discourage the Johnson grass nd also to create a water table for his

planters. He built his walls jigsaw-style, tier on tier, carefully fitting each piece into place, and making sure that each was secure. He finished off his unconventional dry walls at 30 inches—and found he was unable to shake them down.

After filling the bin with a mixture of clay, sand and organic matter, he planted lettuce, radishes, carrots and mustard greens for some off-season fresh salads. It was a simple matter, on nights when frost was predicted, to cover the bin with burlap and newspaper. Meanwhile, his family enjoyed the excellent salad crops—tastier and healthier than the supermarket kind.

California gardener Howard Knapp was doubly miserable when arthritis made it impossible for him to bend over—half from the discomfort and half because it seemed as though his gardening days were over.

But Mr. Knapp had a little workshop, and a lot of ingenuity. Choosing long-lasting redwood lumber, he built a series of boxes, two feet wide and four feet long. Some were eight inches deep, some a foot deep. All were set on 2 x 4 wooden legs so they would be "pants-pocket high."

Placed along a southern wall and filled with rich humus, the boxes are Mr. Knapp's new garden.

He advises making half-inch holes in the box bottoms for drainage, and cautions against watering too vigorously. A soaking hose or gentle watering from a sprinkling can are superior to a "shower" from an

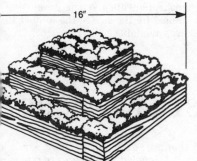
— 16" —

ordinary garden hose that could spatter precious organic material out of the boxes.

Also in California, Vollie Tripp suggested gardening to his wife. "Of course," she said, "but don't expect me to bend over."

Vollie is easy to get along with, so he built her a gardening box, about five feet wide and 16 feet long, with a soil level about 28 inches from the ground—but let's let Vollie describe it in his own words. . . .

It took one day to make—but I'm pretty handy with tools. I don't know how long it will last, but this much I can say—there are no weeds of any kind in that raised garden-box, and there are no insect pests.

Since I had already built a garden box for herbs, I figured there was no reason why a larger box with 7 or 8 inches of soil would not be even more successful. There are many shallow-rooted plants well worth growing to cover costs, so I got going. I found you don't need a blueprint to make a big shallow growing tray filled with choice garden soil.

First I located a cache of 100-year-old hemlock selling at half the price of new, fresh-cut stuff that was thinner and narrower. I bought 10 pieces of 16-foot-long 2 by 8's, and ordered 16 lineal feet of good, sound 4-by-4's which I used as crossties resting on 6 hollow cement blocks.

These were obtained at the local cement plant—each 8-by-8-by-16. I decided to make the box 61 inches wide and 16 feet long, so 7 of the 8-inch planks made a floor with a little spreading to allow for good drainage.

The sides of the box were nailed t the tops of floor planks to give extr soil depth, and a batten was later use to cover the exposed joint.

The crossties or supports were cu from the 4-by-4's in 61-inch lengths– the width of the box. The 6 cemen blocks were set two inches into th ground, the soil was worked in aroun them for good support, and the entir foundation was lined up and mad level. Next, pads were cut from wast lumber, two inches thick and 8 wid and placed on top of the piers. The 4 by-4's were then laid on the pads an nailed lightly into position.

It was simple to lay the floo planking on the crossties, and nai them down with 16-penny stock after fastened the two sides of the box an the outside floor planks togethe Finally, the end sections of the bo were cut to fit, and nailed in place. T prevent spreading at the corners, nailed in a sheetmetal band for extr reinforcement, and also ran a doubl set of #6 wires across the middle fror side to side and twisted them tight t prevent swelling when the wood go wet.

The height of the raised garden—2 inches—is convenient and does r duce bending and stooping. We go for close planting, so there is room for rows or 80 feet of growing room. W find it is easy to reach into the box an do what has to be done. But a dimensions should be up to the folk who will do the gardening. Th measurements given here were deter mined by the size of the lumber tha was available.

A BARREL OF STRAWBERRIES

First, as some joker said, you catch yourself a barrel. This is really the hardest part, since many kinds new-fangled containers are replacin wooden barrels and kegs nowadays.

Perhaps you can still find a lumberyard or hardware store that can give or sell you an old nail keg (nail kegs are so small that you'd want several, if you can get them). Or maybe somewhere in your town, you can find a vinegar barrel. These need to be cleaned out and neutralized with baking soda to prevent the vinegar from giving you unwanted soil acidity.

A very old wooden barrel can look deceptively ratty, with loose staves. Soaking in water for a few days will probably restore it to its original tightness.

With a large, "regular" sized barrel, lay out a ring of six holes on the circumference. Then draw more rings

and lay out more holes, each the same distance apart as the original six holes are from one another, and with six holes in each ring of holes, and staggered as shown in the drawing.

If you have a saber saw, it can be used to make the holes, which should be about two inches in diameter—no larger or the dirt will fall out.

If your shop is really well-equipped, you may have a "hole saw" which attaches to an electric drill and makes faster, neater work of cutting out the two-inch holes. If you don't have a hole saw that's exactly two inches in diameter, use a slightly smaller, rather than a slightly larger one.

Should you be working in a little nail keg, make each ring of holes with only four holes instead of six.

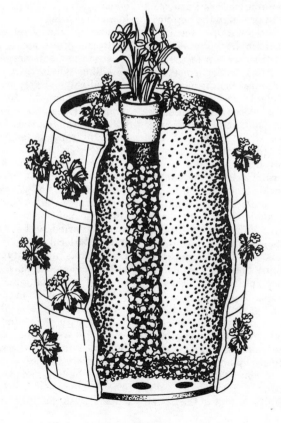

Of course, "making" the barrel is easy. Success—in the form of strawberries—depends on what you do with it. For advice, let's consult John Vivian of Petersham, MI:

The soil should be very rich; an equal mixture of sandy loam, compost and well-rotted manure is ideal. If necessary, you can substitute fine sand, peat and dried manure with liberal amounts of cottonseed meal dug in around the roots. But watch out for the nitrogen content—too much in the spring produces excessive leaf and runner growth, with reduced crops. Cottonseed meal is recommended because it releases its nitrogen slowly, making it available for sustained production.

Drainage and proper positioning of plants are vital to success. Put at least two inches of gravel in the bottom of the barrel, and build up a vertically-ascending core in the center. Pack the soil around the core, up to the first level of planting holes to make an ideal, well-drained rooting medium.

If potted plants are set in the holes, they should be placed inside the barrel with some soil, and the leaves carefully guided out through the hole. Next, push the roots and soil up against the inside of the barrel, working the soil well into the planting hole, and packing more in to fill.

Dormant plants should be set at a downward angle, with both leaves and the crown of the plant protruding from the hole. When packing soil around the roots and into the hole, take care not to bury the crown, which can smother the plant.

Keep adding layers of soil, and building the gravel core until all planting holes contain plants, Then, fill the barrel up with soil and put more plants in the top, leaving at least 8 inches between plants. We put a succession of clay flower pots containing blooming succulents—bulbs or tubers—in the center of the barrel.

This adds a bit of extra color, an when the succulent stems begin droop a bit, we know it's time to wate the barrel.

Strawberries prefer full sun, so th barrel should be left outside in a sunn location. One side of the barrel wi probably shade itself, so the barr should be turned frequently. Turnin is easier if 3 furniture casters ar attached to the bottom before soil an gravel are put in.

After the first spring crop, th plants will produce runners, o stolons, which will grow into nev plants. Since the barrel alread contains as many plants as it can hol these should be pinched off or allowe to root in separate pots. The youn plants can be planted in another barre or used to replace the parent plants th following spring.

In winter, the barrel must be give plenty of protection if left outside because the plants are more expose to killing winds than those grow normally. We simply pack straw o grass clippings around each plant, an wrap the sides and top of the barre with several thicknesses of burlap much the same as tender shrubs ar given winter protection.

If you care as much about straw berries as we do, you can domesticat the wild ones, and get them to grov and produce at home—even in barrels Since the wild berries have a shor ripening period, we have to work fast and get the local youngsters to help us The "barrels" are empty milk carton and ice-cream containers with hole punched in the bottoms and sides— just like the regulation containers.

Then, when the wild plants ar covered with their tiny white an yellow flowers, the kids go ou digging. Wild strawberries grow in nearly every field, woods and vacan lot, are shallow-rooted, and usuall grow in clumps of 3 to 5 plants. Ou helpers dig up clumps about the size o

14

eir hands, pull out the weeds, and
lant them in the "barrels." They use
he same compost and manure-rich
oil we have in the large barrels, and
ith plenty of water and no competi-
on from other plants, the wild berries
re large and more numerous than
hey would be naturally.

We also run a wild berry plot next to
he kitchen where the sandy-loamy
oil is enriched with several winters'
ccumulations of eggshells and coffee
rounds. It gets the full sun, and is host
o a fine collection of red and yellow
iniature salad tomatoes—all volun-
ers. We reasoned that they would
erve as nurses for our wild berry
lants, shading them just as they are in
he field or forest.

So one spring I spaded up the small
atch and went looking for wild
trawberries. I didn't have far to go,
ound a good stand just as the leaves
ere emerging, and dug up several
ozen strong-looking plants, keeping
good spadeful of earth around each
oot cluster.

Wild strawberries are extremely
ardy, and can be transplanted
uccessfully any time up till petal
all—though the earlier, the better.
he smaller strawberries produce 3-
obed, serrated leaves from a single
rown, have white flowers with
ellow centers, and reproduce from
unners, or stolons, like cultivated
lants. They tend to grow in dense
atches in open fields, and are easily
dentified, even before the leaves are
ully out in spring, by the dense mat of
ried leaves and runners that covers
he ground.

After picking out unwanted weeds
-including many smaller strawberry
lants—we set the clumps in on 12-
ach centers, planting exactly as you
vould garden varieties. The bottoms
f the crown were even with the soil
vhich we pressed firmly around roots

that pointed straight down. After
watering, we sat back to wait, and the
results were spectacular!

Following a few days' apparent
shock, the plants began to grow. Soon
the leaves were up to 6 inches across—
more than twice their size in the wild.
Each plant set from 3 to 6 blossoms.
And the berries were giants—most of
them nearly an inch long, and with the
tangy-sweet flavor found only in wild
strawberries. From only a couple of
dozen plants, we picked enough
berries to give that special wild flavor
to a year's supply of strawberry
preserves.

No one has ever defined the cultural
requirements of the wild varieties, so
every gardener is on his own. We have
simply tried to duplicate each plant's
natural environment, only more so.
The improvements—made intentionally or by accident—are nothing but
basic organic principles. Compared to
the purely wild state, our "domesticated" plants enjoy these advantages:

---

*1. Soil with a richer and more
balanced supply of organic nutrients;*

2. More effective mulch;

*3. Consistent and ample water
supply;*

*4. No damaging competition from
other vegetation, through controlled
spacing or mowing.*

Needless to say, insects are no
problem with the tough wild varieties
which require little or no work.

As you can see, John is very fond of
wild strawberries. The same sort of
care applies to domestic varieties.
John tells us he prefers everbearing
varieties like OZARK BEAUTY,
which give him two crops—spring
and fall.

COLD FRAMES

We almost hesitate to suggest ways to make cold frames, because nearly everyone has seen them—and made out of every conceivable kind of materials. Most, of course, begin with some discarded windows. Whatever surplus material is at hand seems to serve as sides, and presto; you've got a cold frame.

Just for fun, let's say you already have a cold frame, and we'll begin with a tip for a simple heater for it. (W worry about things like that here i Pennsylvania where late spring frost are the undoing of many a gardener' dream.) Charles O. Wisham of Bridge ton, NJ, seems to have found th cheapest and quickest way to heat cold frame:

Cold frames are a real help to th gardener, but it is risky placing tende tomatoes and peppers in them here i

New Jersey where the temperatures sag to the 30's and 20's early in April. Here's how I use mine safely when the mercury plummets to 16 or less.

I sank a 5-gallon molasses tin in the center of the 24-by-70-inch frame, leaving the top rim 3 inches above ground level. Into the container I lowered a 250-watt infrared brooder light and hooked it onto the extension plug in the barn. My frame holds about 400 plants, when spotted diagonally two to each 3-inch peat box.

Here are some comparative inside-outside temperature readings taken when the light was on the job:

Outside		Inside
32 degrees		46
26	"	44
22	"	38
16	"	36

The temperatures for the inside were taken from the far ends of the frame. Near the light, of course, they were higher, but they never went below freezing when outside temperatures remained 16 degrees or above.

It's surprising how much cold plants will survive for short periods. By placing the tender tomatoes and peppers near the light, and hardier snapdragons and petunias around the edges, my plants have always come through without damage.

In late April, there will be many times the light is not needed, but it's a simple matter to plug it in when temperatures threaten to fall to the danger point.

As we mentioned earlier, cold frames are made usually from old windows, combined with almost anything else that can serve as sides. One of our favorite "anythings" is hay bales, a tip from Alberta Alexander of Nedrow, NY. The bales are merely laid out lengthwise in rectangles that can be capped by your windows.

Hay makes one of the best possible insulators, and when the cold frame is no longer needed, the hay is efficiently recycled into mulch.

If hay makes the *simplest* kind of cold frame, certainly Pamela Thompson of Brimson, MN, takes the prize for devising the *largest* kind.

The Thompsons have a 25 x 40-foot garden which they find necessary to protect from frosts *during every month of the summer!*

Their answer was to divide the garden into two sections, and cover each during frost warnings with a "giant, economy-sized cold frame." As the diagram shows, it begins with a set of four-foot high posts (2 x 4's are used for these). What look like wires joining those posts in the diagram are really lengths of scrap lumber, with rounded sides to prevent tearing the plastic. At this stage, the Thompsons have a giant frame, high enough to keep the plastic film cover from touching the tops of their vegetables.

They brought a length of four-mil transparent plastic, 16 x 65 feet, and cut it in half to make two pieces, 16 x 32 feet. These were glued together to make a piece 32 x 32 feet, using contact cement.

The big plastic is rolled up and laid by one end of the garden to await a frost warning, or just a family hunch that it may get cold that night.

As you can imagine, it's a two or three-person job to stretch the plastic over the frame and hold its edges down with rocks. But for good organic vegetables' safety, that work is worthwhile. The Thompsons don't even mind crawling under the plastic during a rain and "pushing" the water away so it doesn't burst the plastic.

For sheer ingenuity and versatility, it's hard to beat the "three-in-one" cold frame devised and built by Mrs. O. E. Henderson of Porter, TX. Here's how she did it:

I built it using redwood, which resists ground rot, and it's 12 feet long, four wide, and two feet high in the center. It's wired at top to take electric bulbs that provide extra growing heat

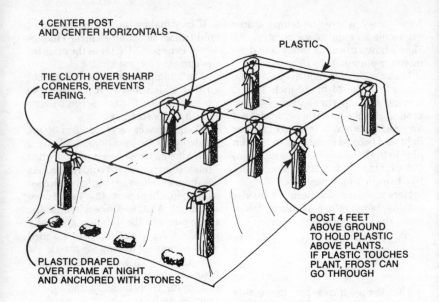

4 CENTER POST AND CENTER HORIZONTALS

PLASTIC

TIE CLOTH OVER SHARP CORNERS, PREVENTS TEARING.

POST 4 FEET ABOVE GROUND TO HOLD PLASTIC ABOVE PLANTS. IF PLASTIC TOUCHES PLANT, FROST CAN GO THROUGH

PLASTIC DRAPED OVER FRAME AT NIGHT AND ANCHORED WITH STONES.

for the young birds and plants.

The frame is still tight and sound, and it makes gardening a lot easier because I prepared the ground first, before moving the frame over the planting site. That's a lot better than trying to work the soil, moving around inside a fixed, immovable frame work. Here are some of the gardening chores and programs it helps me do better:

Around the last of February, I set my tomato and pepper plants, which I have planted in flats and started in the kitchen window, in the cold frame four inches apart in each direction, and cover the frame with clear plastic, so the plants can get plenty of sun. On warm days, I remove the plastic so the plants enjoy some fresh air. They are allowed to stay here for four or five weeks until they are large enough for the garden row. The lights give extra heat, and I use larger bulbs when the weather gets really cold.

After all the plants are out, my double-duty frame now becomes a very efficient chicken house. I put in a good, thick layer of pine straw mulch, and set a clutch of 15 to 20 baby chicks on the litter.

Food and water are placed at one end near a large bulb, and we leave the plastic cover in place, raising one end on sunny days. When the weather gets really warm, we provide shade, using boards and old rugs, which we lay across the top of the frame.

Here's a good garden trick worth trying. When the insects get really active on hot, close nights, we just raise the plastic at one end and—presto!—we have a very effective insect trap. The pests go right through the wire, and the chicks keep eating them all night. No disposal problems—you can't buy a better insect trap.

There is yet another use for my three-in-one frame—as a hotbed to grow fresh greens for the table all winter. But down here in east Texas, we're able to grow our greens all winter.

GREENHOUSES

Let's go from cold frames to greenhouses with a miniature greenhouse built by Betty Brinhart of West Hatfield, MA, which is smaller indeed than many cold frames. Betty describes its use and how she built it:

Because heat gathers quickly within this small house when placed in direct sunlight, no other kind of heat is necessary. Plants do as well here as they do in larger greenhouses, and will continue to grow well in this greenhouse until outdoor transplanting time. To harden seedlings off properly before transplanting, simply lift off the upper section of the greenhouse, and uncover for a few moments longer each day until the plants can take a full day's sun without wilting.

The upper section of the greenhouse may be removed at any time to make watering, weeding and transplanting easier. If you must remove the upper section while the plants are still very young and tender, work in a shaded area so the plants will not be injured by direct rays of the sun or by chilling winds.

Do not put this helpful greenhouse away after the annuals have been removed in June. Remove it to a semi-shaded area, and use it to start biennial and perennial seeds, as well as to root hardwood cuttings. Because high humidity and warmth are so easily maintained within this small house, seeds sprout days ahead of time, and a greater percentage of cuttings root weeks before time.

When you have no further chores for the greenhouse, remove the soil from the planting box and wash the entire structure thoroughly with the garden hose and dry for several days in the warm sun.

Dimensions of the upper greenhouse are optional with the builder. Our miniature greenhouse is twice as long as it is wide, about 36 inches to 18, while the sturdy carrying handles—'E'—are about 61 inches long. The planting box at the bottom is designed to fit snugly inside the handle framework. It is therefore advisable to calculate the dimensions of the different units carefully to ensure a neat, tight outdoor structure. Here's how we built ours.

Upper Section:

Construct two long sides 'A', and two short sides 'B'. Nail or screw together by slipping the shorter sides between the longer. Make two of 'C', and center on top of both shorter sides 'B', making certain the supports for the roof door are on the same side of the greenhouse. Nail or screw in place tightly.

Cut two of 'D.' Before assembling, cut a ¼-inch-deep groove running the length of the lower board on either side of the roof. This groove is cut on the underside so that the roof sections will fit snugly over the top section of the two long sides. Put roof hinges in place and nail the back half of the roof permanently in place, and fasten door hinges to the upper edge of the roof so it will open and close, like a door.

Cut sturdy, clear plastic to fit sides and roof, then tack or staple it in place

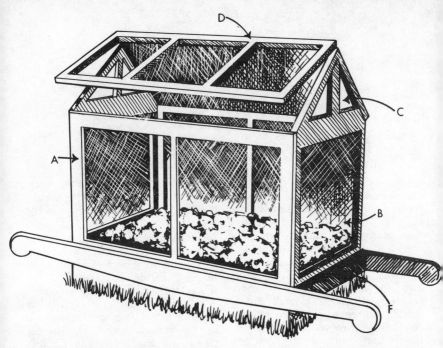

to make the greenhouse airtight. Drill ¼-inch air holes so some air will enter the greenhouse even though the door may be closed.

Lower Section:

Cut two handles and two cross boards to nail in place between the two handles. Boards should be flush with the tops of the handles. You now have a framework that will fit snugly over the actual planting box with handles that enable you to carry the greenhouse indoors at night when temperatures drop too low.

Planting box measurements must be accurate so the box will fit easily into the handle framework. Allow spaces in bottom for good air and water drainage. When finished, slip handle framework over box, and nail in place *one inch* above the lip of the box so that there will be some support for the upper section of the greenhouse. The greenhouse sits right down upon the lip of the planting box, and forms a good seal against outside temperatures.

The entire greenhouse may or may not be painted. If painting is desired, apply an undercoat and top coat of any color of good outdoor house paint. Paint the upper section of the greenhouse before tacking plastic in place. Paint the lower section as soon as completed. Good color combinations to use are bright yellow and dark green.

Much pioneer technology of the early American settlers has not only been resurrected by the people living in communes today; it has often been improved upon by the use of modern materials that our ancestors never heard of. The "Growhole" is such a combination of a primitive pit-style greenhouse with space-age plastic film, devised by the Lama Foundation and used in the southwestern United States.

A Lama factsheet on the Growhole says, "Dig a hole that faces south to catch as much sunlight as possible. Cover it with a membrane that lets the light in but won't let heat out. The dirt walls and floor of the Growhole store

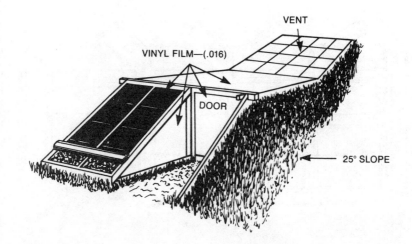

VENT

VINYL FILM—(.016)

DOOR

25° SLOPE

enough heat to keep it warm throughout the night. The hours of daylight and the temperature inside the Growhole mimic a Southern California Valley. Plants that grow well in the Growhole are those that are grown in valleys in Southern California in winter."

These vegetables include lettuce, celery, string beans, carrots, and members of the cabbage family such as broccoli, Brussels sprouts, and cauliflower. Tomatoes and beets don't do as well.

Lama says that the Growhole works best in the southern half of the U.S., south of a line drawn across the country from Big Sur to Norfolk, Va. It may have application north of that line, but its success is dependent on enough sunlight during the day to store heat for the below-freezing nights (temperatures can get to zero in the New Mexican mountains). Without enough daylight sunshine, the Growhole may freeze up at night.

The inventors explain heat economy this way: "The sun radiates about 200 BTU per square foot of the earth's surface during a clear day. About half of this heat is actually collected by the Growhole. A winter's day is about eight hours long and the area of the membrane is about 300 square feet.

"When all of these numbers are combined, we find that 250,000 BTU are collected on a clear winter day. The membrane is two layers of .016-inch vinyl and two layers of Aircap D-120. Aircap is that packing material with the bubbles in it that snaps when you pinch it. Each layer of Aircap is actually two films, so we have a total of six layers.

"On a night when the temperature inside the Growhole is 50 degrees and it's 20 degrees outside, 80,000 BTU are lost through the membranes. But 250,000 BTU were collected. Thus we collect three times as much heat as we're losing. Everything is okay. The plants are growing. . . ."

Lama acknowledges some problems with the Growhole. "The lifetime of this configuration of plastics is unknown. Each layer of Aircap must be hung without the layers above and below touching it. Dew forming on the top layer of plastic blocks light; if the bottom layer was airtight, this might be rectified. Plants must be hand-pollinated due to the absence of wind in the Growhole."

It's worth a try.

In preparing this book, we had to do a lot of soul-searching, and greenhouses gave us the most to think

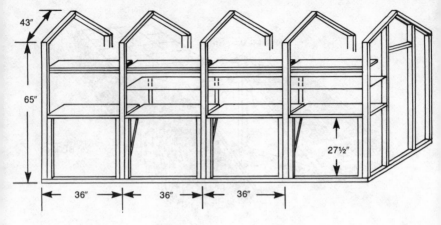

about. We had dozens of articles on hand like the one from Mrs. Margaret Champie, who built a greenhouse for $50 (in 1968) in about three months *when she was 75 years old!*

Mrs. Champie's greenhouse is just a lean-to affair, tacked onto her house with 2 x 4's and covered with plastic film. It serves the purpose admirably, although it might not be some people's idea of a "pretty" greenhouse.

And then, we had some thoughts like: "If a 75-year-old grandmother can build herself a greenhouse, anybody can, so why talk about greenhouses at all?"

Well, the answer is that there are so many possible ways to build a greenhouse (not to mention all the inexpensive kits and ready-made greenhouses) that we'd feel amiss if we didn't point out the many shapes and varieties which are possible to make.

And then a big factor in deciding how *you'll* do the job is what kind of materials are available. Out in Day's Creek, OR, Mrs. Marion Wilbur found the makings in a pile of lumber left after her husband Leonard finished building a livestock stable:

I found a fairly level place, not too far from the house and big enough to accommodate a 12-by-7 structure that

didn't bunk against nearby tree branches.

Fortunately we had a bonanza of leftover lumber, and Leonard conceded that I could use whatever I needed as long as it was less than 6 feet long.

After a weekend of contemplation I was ready to begin. A few long 2-by-4's were "borrowed" from the woodpile and maneuvered around for the floor plan. After the perimeter was determined, I dug a shallow trench and filled it in with pea rock for a base or foundation. The 2-by-4's were then laid on top, leveled, squared and nailed together. (First time in my life I tried to drive a nail through a 2-by-4!) To make sure the corners stayed square, I cut four 90-degree angles from ¾-inch plywood, and nailed them at each corner on top of the 2-by-4's for braces. The maximum height that would clear the tree branches was 85 inches from this base.

With more 2-by-4's, I laid out one of the arches on the patio floor. The correct angles for the roof peak and sides were marked and cut, and used as a pattern to cut 2-by-4's for the rest of the framework. One arch was nailed together, and plywood braces were cut to match the angles where side and roof pieces met, and also at the roof

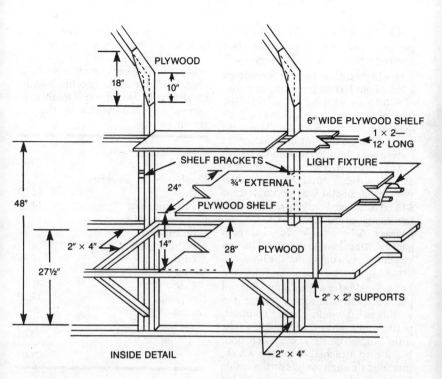

PLYWOOD

18″

10″

6″ WIDE PLYWOOD SHELF

1 × 2—
12′ LONG

SHELF BRACKETS

LIGHT FIXTURE

¾″ EXTERNAL

24″

48″

PLYWOOD SHELF

2″ × 4″

14″

28″   PLYWOOD

27½″

2″ × 2″ SUPPORTS

INSIDE DETAIL

2″ × 4″

peak. These were used again for a pattern to cut enough for the rest of the angles.

Each section was nailed together on the patio floor. Door framing was added to the two ends, which were then carried to the building site, held in position with lightly nailed strips of wood, and then secured in place. A 12-foot-long 1-by-2, nailed to the inside, 48 inches up from the base on each side, secured the arches in their correct spacing, 36 inches apart, and also served as a support for a small 6-inch shelf.

Bench supports and braces were then cut and nailed in position, and external ¾-inch plywood was cut to cover these, notched out around the 2-by-4's. On one side an additional shelf, 8 feet long with a fluorescent light fixture attached to underside, was placed 14 inches above the workbench. This fixture was obtained

along with the lumber from the building we dismantled. Doors and vents were made, hinges attached and hung. A coat of paint over this framework evidently covered a multitude of sins—it was beginning to look pretty good.

At a local building-supply store I found white fiberglass in rolls, 36 inches wide, which seemed much sturdier and more durable than the various plastic coverings I had seen, and sufficiently opaque to diffuse the bright rays of the sun. Enough was purchased to cover the structure for $75.31, including tax. Starting on one side of the building, I unrolled enough to go up over the top and down to the base on the opposite side. This was tacked to the 2-by-4 frame with a staple gun, and then cut off at the bottom with tin snips. Strips of 1-inch redwood lath, which had been painted, were nailed over the edges and seams of the fiberglass. The front panels, door and vents were then covered with sections of fiberglass.

Gro Lights, 8 feet long, ordered from a local light fixture company at a cost of $10.40 were installed, and the light was plugged into a clock timer (left over from a previous appliance) to turn lights on and off automatically. Power was supplied by a 50-foot-long heavy duty cord from an outside outlet at the house. A small electric heater with a thermostat was purchased for $15.50 to be used only on nights when the temperature dropped below 40 degrees. A heat cable would furnish gentle bottom heat to the seed flats and seedlings growing under the light.

Paving bricks were laid on the ground inside for a walk, and a few tall plastic trash containers under the workbench would hold compost, potting mix and other sundries. The little hinged vents above each door had a cord attached to the top which, threaded through eyelets on the inside frame, could be easily opened or closed to adjust air and ventilation. On hot days, both front and back doors could also be open.

Lest we omit a very good source of greenhouse ideas, don't forget that almost every state agricultural extension service can offer plans for the asking. Manfred Holck, Jr., of Springfield, O, wrote to the Cooperative Extension Service of the Virginia Polytechnic Institute in Blacksburg, VA 24061. Here's his experience:

After scrounging around the neighborhood for any used materials I could find, I got the rest from a local lumber dealer.

Since I built the house myself, there were no labor costs. I got the exhaust fan for nothing from a nurseryman who was tearing down a small greenhouse. The door and shelving came out of a condemned house nearby. I installed the gas pipeline, buried a plastic water hose in the same ditch, and put up a 100-foot electric cord, all to connections at my house.

The only ongoing annual cost now, aside from the very small gas bill, is about $20 for replacing the plastic. Plastic will last from October to spring, but deteriorates in the hot summer sun.

My costs were like this—

Lumber, nails, preservative	$ 42.00
Plastic covering	14.50
Gas heater with thermostat	62.35
Electric wire extension cord	12.92
Exhaust attic fan with thermostat	-0-
Gas piping	17.28
Outside door	-0-
Shelving	-0-
Miscellaneous	20.01
	$169.06

I selected a site for my greenhouse near my garden. That way it would be close to where many of the plants would later be transplanted. Furthermore, I need a sunny spot in winter to give warmth and light and yet a reasonably shaded spot in late spring to provide some protection from excessive mid-day sunshine. The sunshine is necessary, of course, but too much on a warm spring day just makes the greenhouse interior too hot.

Once the 12-by-15-foot site was selected, it was leveled and prepared for a foundation. But instead of spending substantial sums on concrete for an adequate base some two feet deep (to get below the frost zone) I improvised with four-by-four-inch posts at the corners and under each rib. Bricks, which had been left over from the construction of our home, were turned on end, without mortar, and packed tightly between posts. This way the foundation could not crack during winter. There was flexibility and movement possible when the ground froze and thawed. Yet, when filled in with earth on both sides, this foundation provided quite adequate support as well as protection from outside cold and field mice.

The actual frame construction of the greenhouse took no more than one weekend once I had all supplies on hand. It was necessary to prepare a "jig" or pattern for the ten rafters. Using the pattern provided by the V.P.I. plans, this was easily done on two large four-by-eight foot sheets of ¾-inch plywood. Each rib was constructed identically out of four pieces of ½-inch by 1⅝-inch by 10-foot strips held together with two-by-four-by-eight-inch spacer blocks glued and nailed in place at designated intervals. Each rib was then cut to identical length and treated with a wood preservative.

Two sets of five ribs each were then spaced equally and attached by wood screws to a two-by-four-inch base-board, 15 feet long, and a one-by-four-inch gable board. The baseboards of both sets of ribs were then nailed on to the four-by-four-inch foundation posts. Two-inch bolts held the two one-by-four-inch gables together.

Framework for the front and back of the greenhouse was constructed from two-by-four-inch studs. The door louvers, fan and heater were set in place. All woodwork was painted with white house paint (and is repainted each year). A double layer of 4-mil polyethylene plastic film was placed on both the underside and topside of the ribs, as well as inside and outside of the front and rear framing. Four-foot lengths of wood lath hold the plastic securely in place. Shelving was placed inside the completed greenhouse with the germination box carefully located under the center shelf. The electric cord was strung and connected, the water hose attached, and the gas line connections completed.

With that, the greenhouse was ready to use!

Perhaps Richard D. Roe of Steubenville, O, didn't have any of that "scrap lumber" lying around that so many of our readers seem to find when they want to build a greenhouse. At any rate, he invested some hard cash and two weeks of spare moments in building a commercially made greenhouse kit. Here's what he ran into:

Seriously considering a greenhouse? Before you take another step, send for as many manufacturers' catalogs as possible. There are now so many models of pre-cut and prefabricated small greenhouses on the market that it pays to shop thoroughly.

Greenhouses differ greatly in methods of construction, size, shape and materials. Some require no foundation, but most do. Choice in materials narrows down to aluminum or redwood for the framework, and glass or plastic for the windows. The framework can be a matter of personal preference, but a truly permanent greenhouse requires glass.

How large should it be? You'll get plenty of planting and growing fun out of the minimal 7 by 10 feet. But if you are really enthusiastic about greenhouse gardening—get the biggest one you can afford because you'll never be satisfied with anything less.

When calculating what your budget will allow, keep in mind that the prices quoted in the catalogs are for the basic structure only. Foundation, heat, water, light, automatic controls, benches and fixtures must be built or purchased separately.

Most important is whether you do the labor yourself or hire outside help. In my case, doing it all and paying for no outside labor kept the final cost of the completely equipped greenhouse down to *about double the price of the basic* structure!

My 9-by-12-foot redwood and glass house went up in just two weeks, although I worked only a few hours in the evenings and on weekends—with part of the time off for rain, and nearly half the rest of it consumed by the painting required. The remaining work of installing benches, heat and the numerous miscellaneous jobs required another week.

Both heat and water can come from the main residence, if you build a wing or an extension. But if you don't, the buildings should be as close together as possible to make travel between them easy in all kinds of weather. And, of course, the greenhouse should be placed to get as much sunlight as possible all year.

A greenhouse should be built from the start to handle and live with lots of water and dampness or humidity. This is why only the natural rot-resistance of redwood or aluminum is suitable. Even then, two or three coats of paint are advised for redwood. It is also why the right floor is most important. A greenhouse floor is not simply a pathway, but also contributes to growing conditions for plants and to the comfort and safety of those who work and visit there. It cannot be a solid slab of concrete, nor even stones or bricks laid in concrete, because it must permit rapid drainage of water.

Wood in any form has no place there. Apart from its rapid disintegration from constant moisture, wood that remains wet for long periods becomes as slippery as ice. Flagstones laid dry on a bed of sand may be used, or the flat concrete slabs now available for patios. My own final choice of red rough bricks provides the surest possible footing and the desired rapid drainage.

The floor covers only the center aisle. The area directly beneath the benches is covered by a two-inch layer of sand over bare soil which allows the water to drain to a corner where a small pipe conducts it through the foundation wall to the ground outside. Such a floor both conveys excess water away, and also provides a porous surface that may be wetted down frequently to maintain necessary humidity.

Before you buy and install heating equipment decide what type greenhouse you will operate. Plants may be divided into three groups, depending on their reactions to greenhouse conditions. The cool house with a temperature range of 45-60 degrees, is easiest for the beginner.

There are many plants that thrive in such temperatures during the winter, and some that actually require this coolness. Flowers for winter include snapdragons, calendulas, candytuft, bachelor's buttons, and geraniums (pelargoniums). Vegetables such as lettuce, spinach and radishes, and a host of bulbous plants including such exotics as veltheimia, sparaxis, ixia and others too tender for outdoor growth, are ideally suited to the cool greenhouse. This temperature range is also ideal for forcing spring bulbs. This is the least critical temperature range; a rise to 70 or 75 during sunny weather, and a drop to 40 on the coldest nights does no harm.

The intermediate greenhouse, of moderate warmth ranging from 55 to 65 or 70 degrees, accommodates the greatest range of plants. Almost all annuals and many of the true exotics from subtropical regions thrive in this temperature range.

The warm greenhouse, ranging from 60 to 80 or 85, with a humid atmosphere, is required for most plants from tropical regions, as well as many of the supreme aristocrats—the orchids. The tropical greenhouse is not practical for the small dimensions of most home greenhouses in northern climates because it is very difficult to maintain temperatures within the necessary close tolerances.

The average greenhouse owner will

find that the cool or intermediate house best suits his requirements. The former is especially ideal for the gardener interested in vegetables, and in the later-winter start of the outdoor garden from seeds. The cool greenhouse does a good job of producing the stocky, sturdy seedlings that thrive best when transplanted to the open garden and which yield the earliest returns. Even in the cool house, with the previously described factors governing my own heating equipment, I find that tomatoes and peppers grow rapidly and well when planted in a bench near the heater where the night temperature is 5 to 10 degrees warmer than the farthest corner with its minimum of 45 degrees.

The single most important factor in installing heat is to allow a considerable margin of safety according to the climate prevailing in your area.

Any ordinary room heater will warm your greenhouse satisfactorily during the cold months. You don't have to install expensive equipment to heat the benches or go in for fan-forced heat. I don't recommend the even heat distribution a fan provides. As long as you've got the necessary minimum temperature in all parts of the greenhouse, the uneven warmth of a gravity forced heater creates different heat levels, permitting the growing of plants of different classes in the same house. I find that I can operate both a cool greenhouse and, in a more limited area, an intermediate temperature for plants that thrive in a higher temperature. As an example, selection of locations allows such diverse plants as freesias, lettuce, pelargoniums, coleus and tomatoes to thrive in the same 9 by 12 house at the same time.

Using electricity, gas or oil will be based on availability, cost and ease of installation. Any system you install will, of course, be operated by a thermostat. In some cases, the heating system of the main house can be extended to the greenhouse. Electricity has its advantages, but is very expensive. If gas or oil is used, the heater must be vented to the outdoors because the fumes are lethal to plants. When your heating system is ready, test some tomato seedlings which are among the first to succumb to fuel fumes.

Proper provision for adequate ventilation and shading are absolutely essential to successful greenhouse management. As the sun gains strength in the spring and through the summer, it generates almost unbelievable heat when passing through clear glass. Most small greenhouses come equipped with just one roof ventilator, covering no more than 10 per cent of the roof area, and additional ventilators are usually optional at extra cost. So skimp somewhere else and spend the extra money on enough ventilators to extend the length of the roof at least on one side—which should be away from prevailing winds. I find that a greenhouse cannot have too much air circulation—avoiding direct wind. It is necessary not only to allow excess heat to escape, but also to admit fresh air for plant health.

At least one of the ventilators must be operated by automatic equipment to adjust air circulation according to the inside temperatures unless the greenhouse is given continual daytime observation. Mine is a self-contained unit that expands and contracts with enough power to raise a 15-pound load. While this is considered a mere "gadget" in large establishments and by most experienced glasshouse gardeners, I have found it effective and reliable.

The type of shading required depends largely on the varieties of plants grown in the greenhouse during the warmer months. Sunloving plants such as chrysanthemums, carnations and many annuals do best with a shade that admits considerable light while excluding the sun's harmful rays. This can be a shading compound painted directly on the glass or tinted plastic attached to it.

The tropicals and colorful begonias and achimenes demand denser shade. Roll-up shutters of bamboo or cedar, while relatively expensive to buy, are reasonably permanent. Since they are attached to the outside of the glass, they reduce heat considerably and do an outstanding job under the variable light conditions of spring and autumn when an intermittent and flexible shading program is necessary.

Here in eastern Ohio, just about opposite Philadelphia, I allow the sun to shine through the sides of the greenhouse in early morning and late afternoon, but shade the entire roof area and part of the south side. During the summer season, the shades remain permanently down and, of course, are securely tied against thunderstorms.

Should you install permanent soil-filled benches, or extend the growing of plants to pots, baskets, tubs, flats, and other portable containers? In the small greenhouse, I consider soil-filled benches too limiting. After a year of operation, when the more permanent plants have gained size, and especially if many seedlings are started in spring, finding space for everything in relation to light and heat requires continuous shifting of containers.

While there are disadvantages to container growing, I have found that the advantages far outweigh them in growing a greater variety and number of plants. *Portable containers permit that greatest advantage of shifting plants to various locations to determine where they will thrive best in a small greenhouse. This I would not be without!* In rare cases, such as carrots or radishes, where a larger soil mass is desired, I build a deep flat of larger-than-normal dimensions, and install it in some part of the regular bench

where it can be dismantled when the crop has been harvested, or can even be moved about if assistance is available.

Cultivation of plants in pots requires more critical attention to watering and feeding, but the compensation in manueverability outweighs this minor inconvenience. In the small greenhouse, benches would be justified only if a few specialized crops were to be grown—lettuce and spinach; snapdragons, carnations or chrysanthemums. If such a specialty is to occupy part of the space, one side of the house might have a permanent bench, with the other side for portable containers. In either case, the benches must support a tremendous weight. Construct them accordingly.

Every greenhouse requires two main work areas. Plenty of soil, plus the ingredients for making potting mixtures—sand, peat and fertilizers—must be handy. There must be a table for potting, a shelf or cabinet for storing empty pots, labels and the miscellaneous items of any greenhouse operation. And there should be a table in an out-of-the-way corner kept perfectly dry for use as a desk, for some sort of record-keeping is a distinct advantage in growing plants everywhere.

It helps especially to know when plants are first potted, when re-potted, and when fertilized. If a variety of plants is grown, it is soon apparent that the separate kinds respond differently to various methods, including frequency of fertilizing and light placement. Notes of the most vital statistics are a great help in maintaining plants in good condition and for future reference.

There are no "secrets" to the successful operation of a greenhouse, but there are some rules you'll have to respect—or you'll run into a lot of trouble. Here they are, in short, handy order:

1—Work with potting soil that drains well and yet contains lots of organic matter—plain garden soil is not suitable.

2—Run a water pipe into the greenhouse—you'll need it. When you water, be thorough and then wait until the soil surface is dry to the touch; and be sure to humor the particular demands of the individual plant.

3—An abundance of fresh air is vital; open the ventilator just a bit even when the temperature is quite low.

4—Be absolutely clean at all times!

Remove dead plants and pots of old soil; empty all trash containers frequently; scrub the entire interior at least once a year—usually in June and—better do it again in October.

The yearly cost of operating the

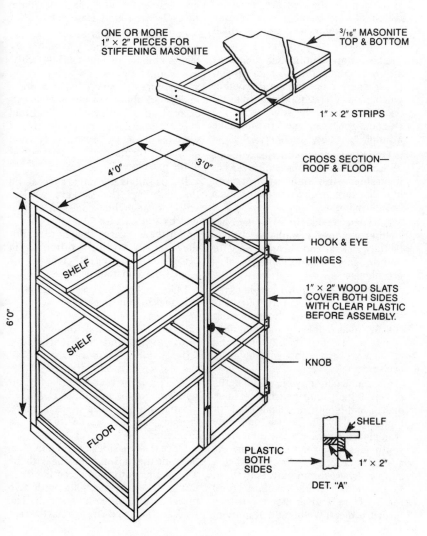

ONE OR MORE 1" × 2" PIECES FOR STIFFENING MASONITE

³/₁₆" MASONITE TOP & BOTTOM

1" × 2" STRIPS

CROSS SECTION— ROOF & FLOOR

4'0"

3'0"

6'0"

SHELF

SHELF

FLOOR

HOOK & EYE

HINGES

1" × 2" WOOD SLATS COVER BOTH SIDES WITH CLEAR PLASTIC BEFORE ASSEMBLY.

KNOB

SHELF

PLASTIC BOTH SIDES

1" × 2"

DET. "A"

average small greenhouse will be a minor factor in your budget. Electricity for light and water is inexpensive. Heat is the largest expense, but in the coldest months my cool 9-by-12 greenhouse uses no more than 6 dollars worth of natural gas per month. The only other expense, aside from the expendables associated directly with gardening (fertilizer, peat, etc.), is the cost of a new coat of paint every two or three years. Not even counting the pleasure derived—which is considerable—the returns from the greenhouse more than offset the expenses.

Okay, now; supposing you can't afford a commercially-made greenhouse and for one reason or another you can't or won't build one—it's still possible to enjoy the advantages of a greenouse on a small scale if you make a simple "window greenhouse."

Jane Stuwe of Great Falls, Mt., has all kinds of greenhouses all over her homestead—free-standing, tacked onto the garage, and what she calls a "winter window."

Let's just consider how she made her "winter window" greenhouse. It may be the quickest and cheapest way for you to enjoy the advantages of a greenhouse:

It's situated on the west side of the house, and sits securely over the window, but can be easily removed. It cost $25, was finished in one summer's spare time, is 4 feet high, 2½ wide, and 18 inches deep, with two shelves on each side.

For construction we used 3 lengths of 1-by-8-inch lumber each 8 feet long, one 10-foot length, and 6 pieces of 10-foot-long 1-by-4's. A used window was placed on the west, while on the south glass was cut and fit in the casing. Scrap 2-by-4's formed the support where the window is attached to the house, while insulation and roofing were leftover material from a former project. We bought aluminum

brackets, 4-lag screws, nails and putty, but the inside shelves were cut from used 1-by-8's. This window structure can be adjusted to any size window.

For $45—and that includes a $20 heater—Mike and Sylvia Becker built themselves a highly effective plastic unit that sits on the back porch of their home in Far Rockaway, New York. It took them one weekend to do the job, and it now gives them a 12-month growing season, which includes tomatoes all-year-round. Here's how:

Building materials include six 12-foot lengths of ordinary 1-by-2's; six pieces of 3/16-inch masonite—two 4-by-6's and four 3-by-4's— three small strap hinges, a small wooden doorknob, and about ten yards of heavy clear plastic sheeting, plus a hook and eye, screws, nails and tacks. If you want to cut costs, you can use plywood at about 19 cents a square foot instead of the masonite.

It's also advisable not to cut costs on the sheeting. The Beckers worked with Clopane which comes in 54-inch widths and sells for 80 cents a yard—$8 for the ten yards they needed. But they feel it's worth the difference in price—the flimsy polyethylene doesn't stand up to constant wear.

Mike Becker's big "secret" in saving time was to build one panel at a time—seven were needed—starting in with the sides. The 1-by-2 stripping was cut into two 6-foot and four 3-foot lengths. After making a frame of them, he cut the plastic to fit, and attached a 3-by-6-foot piece to each completed unit with tacks or a stapling gun. He tacked plastic on both sides of each frame, creating an air space to act as insulation.

Once the two sides were completed, he made the roof and flooring with the 3-by-4 masonite, again creating insulating space by working with two pieces of masonite on each unit. The back section (that sits against the rear wall) is also made of double panels of 4-by-6 masonite, packed with insulating material like rock wool. If you prefer windows in the rear, just frame out a back section of 1-by-2's with two sheets of clear plastic.

It is important—however fast you want to get on with the job—to make the sections so they fit tightly. No air should leak or filter in, and you should be able to control inside temperatures within predictable limits. So the two front panels—one will serve as the door—should fit very snugly. Work with two 6-foot and four 2-foot pieces of 1-by-2's for each panel, tacking the plastic over the framework, and attaching the strap hinges and other necessary fittings later.

After all your panels are ready, it's best to join them with #4 screws instead of nails. Connect the two sides to the bottom and top, and then attach the back. When you have a good, firm framing, add the two front panels, putting the door hinges to one side. The final steps are to cut shelves, and fit them into place by securing small blocks of wood inside the framework. You can now paint, stain or coat the assembled greenhouse—or leave it as it is.

The electrical ceiling outlet is inexpensive and easy to install. It should consist of a socket for a 30-watt bulb plus the connection for the heater plug.

You'll find a whole host of uses for this handy porch greenhouse. It's good for tender plants over the winter, and also for starting seedlings for next year's garden. You can even grow tomatoes and lettuce all winter. A southeast exposure seems best for maximum light and, with a little self-help and study, you'll find yourself depending on and using your porch greenhouse for many years to come.

GEODESIC GREENHOUSE

Did you ever wonder why people get so hung up on geodesic domes? Well, it's because of all the forms you can use to create a container (cylinders, cubes, pyramids, etc.) the sphere, or hollow ball, is the most "efficient." That means it can contain the most space while using the least material in the container, and that for a given material, you can build a stronger container in a spherical shape than any other.

(Mother Nature discovered this long before we did. Many bird eggs are nearly spherical. Chicken eggs and others which have evolved to the typical "egg" shape were Mother Nature's modification to keep the eggs from rolling away if they were laid on flat areas, or to make them "fit" closer together if laid in a nest.)

And the geodesic dome is the nearest thing the average man can build that approaches a perfect sphere, or a portion of one. We saved this one for last, because it's the hardest to build. But if you like "strange" shapes in your backyard, and if you'd like to explain to the neighbors how efficient the spherical shape is, read how Knight Starr of Mount Shasta, Ca., built a "dome" greenhouse for a little more than $25:

Don't underestimate the strength and utility of the six-sided hexagon which Nature uses in the honeycomb to provide stability, while even the gentle snowflake is invariably a six-pointed star. If you look at the sketches you will note that triangles, laid together, make up the domes of our greenhouse.

To construct ours we bought $10 worth of six-mil polyethylene sheeting and were lucky enough to cut 500

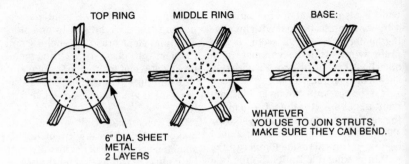

TOP RING   MIDDLE RING   BASE:

6" DIA. SHEET
METAL
2 LAYERS

WHATEVER
YOU USE TO JOIN STRUTS,
MAKE SURE THEY CAN BEND.

feet of the necessary wood struts from one-by-two-inch grape stakes—all gratis. Such wood will cost about three cents a foot in most mills. The dome is about 12 feet in diameter and eight high, while the ceiling is made up of 12 five-foot struts. The others are all three feet long, except for the top horizontal ring (see sketch) which is made of 28-inch boards. The door and frame are made of two-by-fours with the vertical members running down into the ground where they are held rigid by diagonals and rocks.

The dome is supported by 12 two-by-four blocks set under the bottom horizontal ring. We placed a small fan in one of the windows for ventilation, a small smudge pot or heater helps fight frost, and we have left a small hole in the center of the ceiling for a removable stovepipe chimney—all aids to temperature control. Circular racks in the interior support flats or pots and make for effortless watering by a standard radial garden sprinkler.

CEILING: Cut 12 five-foot lengths of one-by-twos, and 12 more 28-inch lengths of the same. Use a mitre-box or table saw to cut all wood with 60-degree ends which makes for tight joints, and paint all wood before you start construction. We joined our boards by using doubled six-inch-wide aluminum sheet metal disks cut from roofing material. Holes in the disks were drilled before assembling —screws were used in the ceiling, and barbed nails were used in the walls.

First join the 28-inch pieces in a line (see sketch), and then attach the five-foot lengths, and then bring the assembly into a ring. It's a good idea to get a friend or neighbor to lend a hand here—you'll need it. We secured the five-foot boards in the center of the ceiling by joining two boards at a time with a sheet metal plate, then joining another pair by using another over-lapping plate, and thus continued all the way around, leaving the hole in the center for the chimney.

WALL: We cut 72 three-foot struts, painted them, and then gave them 60-degree ends. Next we cut the sheet metal disks for the 12 vertices or meeting places on the middle ring where six supports meet, and 12 for the bottom ring where four boards meet (again, see sketch). Cut the holes in the disks in advance, two holes for each wood support. When lining the struts with the disks, mark the wood exactly to fit the holes in the disks and then drill holes to avoid splitting.

Lay out the entire wall on the lawn and assemble. Then, with the welcome help from friends, raise the completed ceiling assembly and support its center about five feet above the ground on a ladder. Then, bring the wall upright, and circle it around so you can connect it to the ceiling with screws to create the dome. The door frame is installed last after you have placed your greenhouse on its permanent site.

POLYETHYLENE: A six-by-100-foot roll of six-mil polyethylene sells

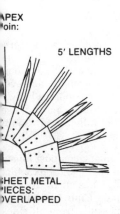

5' LENGTHS

SHEET METAL
PIECES:
OVERLAPPED

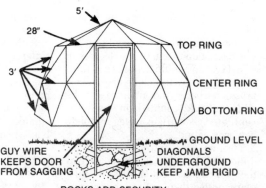

5'

28"

3'

TOP RING

CENTER RING

BOTTOM RING

GROUND LEVEL

GUY WIRE
KEEPS DOOR
FROM SAGGING

DIAGONALS
UNDERGROUND
KEEP JAMB RIGID

ROCKS ADD SECURITY

or about $8. We took tarpaper to make an exact outline of each triangle and used it to cut out the plastic with a razor and straightedge. Allow overlap to compensate for errors and to cover the vertices. We doubled the ceiling layers because of snow and severe weather conditions prevailing in this area, and also suggest laying the plastic on stretched chicken wire will make an even more durable ceiling. A staple gun will secure the sheeting to the wire, while quarter-inch staples will secure it to the struts. Finally, leave a little extra plastic for the bottom triangles so it will cover the ground and keep the cool air out.

COMPOST HEAPS AND CONTAINERS

If there's a lot of variety in the different ways people build greenhouses, there are ten times as many ways in which people build compost heaps—pits, boxes, or cages. Remembering that the sky's the limit in your ingenuity, here is a sampling of some of the ways our readers have devised for turning garbage into rich, moist humus. But first let's look at some of the "old standby" ideas that have been around so long that we can't remember who invented them:

Back in 1961 Lyman Wood built the wire and wood bin shown here using scrap two-inch-square lumber, which he covered with half-inch chicken

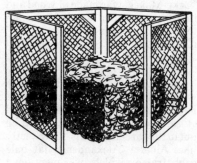

wire mesh for a total cost of $4. Made of two L-shaped sections held together with screendoor hooks, the cage provided him with 18 to 24 cubic feet of finished compost in 14 days, which was par for the composting course then.

Composter Wood reported that the pile heated up to 140 to 160 degrees in two days, and could be turned in four. He damped down each layer—leaves, grass, garbage and manure—as he added it, and counted on the well-ventilated cage to encourage complete bacterial action.

Turning was extremely easy. He unhooked the sides, separated each of the L-shaped sections, and then reassembled them next to the square-sided heap. "You will be pleasantly surprised at how neatly and firmly the heap stands," he wrote, adding: "It is now a simple and satisfying task, using a fork, to peel the layers off the pile and toss them in the now-empty cage." During the turning operation, he kept a hose handy to wet down the heap as the material was transferred.

"I have used this cage many times," he concludes, "for 14-day rapid composting, and each time it is a satisfying successful venture to harvest the cube of dark, moist, crumbly humus."

The same idea—a portable compost bin that can be lifted, leaving a pile ready for turning—was used about six years ago by the Peter Seymour Company of Hopkins, Minnesota. The "Cake-Maker" was made of wood and metal framing, and was light enough to be lifted off the pile, leaving a "cake" of compost, and ready to be filled again.

* * *

Alden Stahr once made an all-winter compost bin out of old bales of hay stacked around secondhand storm doors and windows which he put in the garden. (This is built exactly like Alberta Alexander's hay-bale cold frame, which we mentioned earlier. It's just that the use is different.) Composter Stahr mixed in garbage and manure to help heat up the pile, while the glass lid—slanted to the south to pick up the long, low, midwinter rays of the sun—also kep out scavenging cats and dogs.

Although he recorded a 50-degree difference in temperatures between the inside of the bin and the outdoors one cold January morning, he achieved an extra supply of compost, which he had ready for early-spring use "thanks to the billions of happy bacteria hard at work."

* * *

The classic among compost bins is the wooden New Zealand box which was originally designed by the Auckland Humic Club to admit as much air as possible from all sides. Many variations exist—so don't hesitate to change your design to fit your material and budget.

The important factor is air circulation and ventilation from all sides, so be sure to leave one-inch spaces between your slats or boards. It's a good idea to start with a rugged framework—two-by-fours are excellent—and then nail a lattice of boards over it. The top and bottom are left open, although some composters prefer to cover the top of the pile in rainy weather to prevent leaching. One or two good coats of linseed oil should be allowed to soak into the wood to make it weather- and rot-resistant.

* * *

West Coast gardener John Meeker reported several years ago how he solved the twin problems of running a compost pile in a congested suburban area without offending his neighbors while getting enough compost to run his garden. He circulated air into the heap, using a steel drum which cost him $1, and had it raised six inches of the ground by setting it up on a circular metal frame with legs. Meeker's frame, worth $15 if done in a commercial shop, cost him nothing. But other readers have set their steel drums on eight-inch cement blocks which get them up into the air for practically nothing.

Meeker reported that "the construc

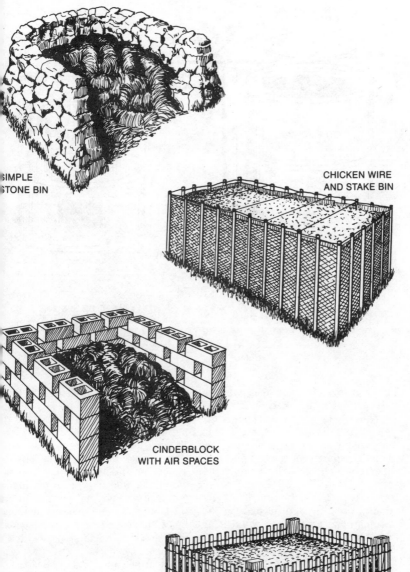

SIMPLE
STONE BIN

CHICKEN WIRE
AND STAKE BIN

CINDERBLOCK
WITH AIR SPACES

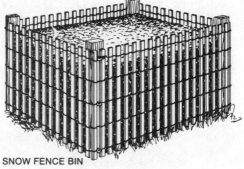

SNOW FENCE BIN

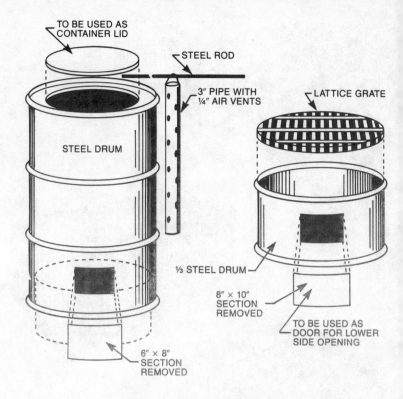

TO BE USED AS CONTAINER LID

STEEL ROD

3" PIPE WITH ¼" AIR VENTS

STEEL DRUM

LATTICE GRATE

⅓ STEEL DRUM

8" × 10" SECTION REMOVED

TO BE USED AS DOOR FOR LOWER SIDE OPENING

6" × 8" SECTION REMOVED

tion has several advantages over the piles and pits that I used before. *The air can circulate up from the bottom of the barrel.* The six-inch space allows easy removal of the compost. The moisture content of the compost can be carefully regulated by covering the barrel with a lid ... leaching of the compost is perfectly controlled. *By simply covering and uncovering the top, one can regulate the amount of air introduced into the mass."*

There is always a bushel or two of compost ready, Meeker noted, even with so small a composter "once the cycle has begun." This includes such seasonal bonuses as summer grass clippings, autumn leaves and crop residues which are "ready to enrich the garden by the time one gets ready for spring planting."

As for the neighbors "who have gladly shared" my bumper harvests

while "turning up their noses at my deposits of leaves, cuttings, manure and—worse—garbage," Meeker reported solution of the odor problem. "When I have a large amount of lettuce leaves, beet tops, grass cuttings or kitchen refuse, *I whiten the top of the dampened pile with a sprinkling of ground limestone,* and over that I add a thick layer of dried steer manure. *The limestone helps to decrease the smell and lessen the acidity of the green refuse and garbage."*

A more complicated application of the steel-drum composter calls for nesting one drum on the bottom third of a slightly larger container, and installing a metal lattice grate between them to hold the pile up so air can get at it. Built by Ralph Poe of Canton, Illinois, the drum composter also featured a hollow, vertical, three-inch-wide pipe with quarter-inch perforations that was thrust down into the heap's center and left there for additional ventilation, as shown in the accompanying diagram.

When a dedicated composter decides to automate his pile, all sorts of Rube Goldberg contraptions may result. Each has a distinct personality according to the personality of its maker and the sort of materials that were available when he made it. We have tried to select the simplest revolving-drum composter, and the one made from materials that you are most likely to be able to obtain.

A warning—the basic element here is a 50-gallon drum. In many cases, the drum will formerly have been used to contain an oil, detergent, solvent or other industrial materials that won't make a welcome addition to your compost pile. So devote a lot of time to making sure that your drum is thoroughly free of its former contents before you start assembling a compost maker out of it.

Our choice of the simplest possible drum composter is the one made by Julian E. Fletcher of Santa Cruz, Ca.:

I'm proud of the drum composter that I built in about 8 hours, and that cost me (see table of itemized cost) $12.15.

As the illustration shows, it sits diagonally on a 1¾-inch pipe 42 inches above the ground, which makes it easy to get a two-wheel garden cart under it for quick loading. The supporting pipe is 50 inches long, and measures 47 inches between the 2-by-4, 58-inch-long posts that are set 18 inches in the ground.

The drum itself is a conventional 50-gallon metal container with a lid cut from the filling end, which is securely locked into place with 1½-by-5-inch metal strips or cleats. The supporting pipe passes diagonally through the center of the drum, and is welded to it at each end. The wood turning handle at the bottom end consists of two 1-by-3-inch crossed boards which are bolted to the flange on the end of the pipe.

The illustration should give you a fairly clear idea of how my drum composter works. Here's how I put it together:

ITEMIZED COSTS FOR DRUM COMPOSTER

One 50-gallon drum	$ 3.50
Length of 1¼-inch pipe	1.50
1¼-inch pipe flange	.50
10-foot post, 2-by-4 inches	1.25
½-by-3-by-5-inch board	.50
8 bolts	.40
welding	3.50
white paint for drum inside	1.00
	$12.15

First, I cut an oblong 1¾-by-3-inch hole 3½ inches from each end of the drum, through which I passed the 1¾-inch pipe which was threaded on one end only. I started pushing the unthreaded end through the drum after marking off 6½ inches from the threaded end with a hacksaw, and kept going until the mark made contact just at the hole where I welded the pipe to the drum all around and then repeated the operation.

The drum and pipe were now secured to each other, and notches

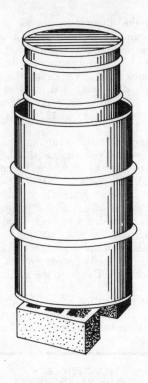

were cut into the supporting posts which were set 46 inches apart, from center to center, plumb and level from top to top. The notches were cut 1⅝ inches from the top, rounded and smoothed, and lined with graphite grease. Before slipping the pipe into place, I put a 1¾-inch large cut washer over the threaded end, and made a turning handle by crossing two 3-by-27-inch boards which I fastened to a 1¼-inch pipe flange with 3 two-inch bolts. I then screwed the flange up as snug as I could to the end of the pipe, slid the large cut washer toward the post, and secured it by drilling a 3/16-inch hole through the pipe and then thrusting a large nail clear through the pipe and bending it slightly. This washer removes all end-play.

The removable lid which is cut out of one end of the drum is held in place by a 1-by-3-inch board plus the metal cleats.

After moving to a retirement hom in Cantonment, Fl., Bette Wahlfeld found her organic gardening styl cramped slightly for lack of space.

She adapted to the situation with portable, knock-down compost bin:

A movable compost bin comes i handy down here in northern Florid where we have plenty of clos neighbors and only one acre of land As we built it, our bin will fit into eve the smallest city plot.

To make it, we cut ten-foot-long one-by-ten-inch boards into five-foo lengths, slotting each board fou inches in from the end, and then fiv inches across its width so they coul be "nested," as shown in the illustra tion. When we finished, we had made 51-inch square bin, 30 inches high, an quite easy to move about.

It took us one hour to make ou highly useful compost bin, and w spent $7.50 for the lumber.

We are happy to report that our ne bin is already paying for itself. In si weeks, our kitchen refuse, plu gathered leaf mold and pine needle (abundant hereabouts) are alread producing usable compost. Pensacol may be blessed with beautiful sand but we organic gardeners know tha sand can always be improved both i texture and nutritional value b compost—made by our movable bin.

A compost container that caugh our fancy for its ingenuity an simplicity is that of Leon R. Horsted o Waunakee, Wi. It takes a length o snow fencing, some hardware clot (wire screening with ½ or ¼ inc

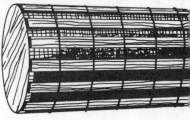

mesh) and two round pieces of wood to make the ends, as shown in the illustration.

Turning your pile in this container requires only an occasional kick to roll it around.

Emptying it can consist of merely rolling it along over the garden area and letting the material sift out. Large pieces of material that won't sift out can merely be left in to break down with the next load of compost that's made in it.

Mr. Horsted suggests that the whole thing could be suspended on a piece of horizontal pipe, like a chicken on a rotisserie, for handy rotation. And we might add that doing this will enable you to sift out the finest compost for use with your house plants, should you desire.

POOLS AND PONDS

A lot of people feel that a homestead isn't *really* a homestead unless there's a glint of water visible somewhere on the landscape. We agree.

Going first-class with a pond measured in acres can be quite a hassle and involve a lot of money for bulldozers, etc. So let's go at it from the simple end, and look first at the world's smallest lily pool—made by Mary Alice Roche of Caldwell, N.J., from an old washtub:

Total costs came to $7—$2 more for sky-blue water-resistant paint. The entire job took us two days, and could have been done in one. One important chore that we did in advance was to thoroughly wipe the inside of the shiny new tub with vinegar, which helps bond the paint to the metal so it doesn't peel off later.

We dug the hole for our pool in one corner of the terrace, about the size of the tub. Plenty of earth was kept nearby for fill—in and around the tub—it always takes much more than you think. Naturally, soil for the pool was enriched with compost. The bottom of the hole was made flat and smooth, and checked with a level. When the tub was set in place, we rechecked by placing the level across it on a board—first in one direction and then in another—to prevent tilting of the tub after it was filled with soil and water. Even a slight tilt can be troublesome.

The hole around the tub was filled with soil, up to about two inches below the rim, leaving room for an edging of bricks. These were alternated, a whole brick with a half-brick, so they would fit smoothly around the circular tub. Bed and crevices between the bricks were then packed with soil.

The effect might have been more interesting if irregular stones had been used, with some extending over the edge of the pool. But this would have made winter protection difficult; keeping the pool level with the bed made it easier to cover with a board. As it was, the edge of the tub was left slightly above its surroundings, so soil would not wash into it during a rainstorm.

The tub itself was filled halfway to the top; first with an inch of sand; then an inch of rotted cow manure (waterlilies like to be well fed); then a 3-inch layer of rich garden soil, and an inch more of sand to keep the water clear. The manure was placed at the bottom so it would not discolor the water. Weighted down with stones, a burlap bag was placed over the sand and soil to keep them from becoming disturbed when water was added.

Admittedly our pool *was* small, and we did want the water to show. So we selected a single small but lovely waterlily *Colorata* because its dainty leaves and delicate pale-blue flowers would spread out to make a charming pattern. Two plants would have completely covered the water and spoiled the effect.

To make sure our miniature pool remains the center of attraction, all other summer plants were subordinated to it—competing forms or colors were avoided intentionally. Fluffy, low, white and lavender alyssum was grown around the front, while the bed in back was filled with rosy, tiny-leaved coleus, some sprigs of which were permitted to invade the rigidly severe circle of the pool.

In the fall, tulips and daffodils were tucked in the bed, to be joined—when they flowered in the spring—by primroses and violas around the edge of the tub. In this way there was plenty of color until our tender waterlily could be replaced for another season of bloom.

We're rather pleased with our pleasant and modest pool which has added so much variety and interest to our garden with so little work and without straining the family budget.

We have a friend and correspondent named Brian Furner in Kent, England, who insists you can build a nifty pool for your garden in just two hours! Well, maybe the English build pools faster than we do it in Emmaus. At any rate, here is Brian's recipe for a quick one:

Modern pool-making is dead-easy. In the old days, it was hard work, and the easiest part was digging out the hole! Hours were spent hammering in a firm base, mixing concrete, and then racing desperately to get the job done before dark. Finally, the pool had to be filled and emptied repeatedly before you could introduce fish and plantlife.

How much better it is today! I use string to mark out the excavation, and after the hole is dug, I lay a tough but flexible lining material—a butyl rubber sheet is fine—fill with water, and then plant my aquatics.

Two Hours to Dig
A 9-Foot-Square Pool

It took me just two hours to dig and line my 9-foot-square pool with a 12-foot-square butyl rubber sheet which cost me $57. Black or blue polyethylene is fine for temporary pools, but I prefer the tougher material for finish jobs.

Since your pool should harmonize with the general surroundings, I advise doing a little advance thinking before digging. While an 18-inch depth is about right, some folks prefer two feet. Heat of the pool can also be important—a tiny pool is liable to be too hot for your fish in the summer and you may have to move them indoors if your winters are long and cold.

Beware of too much shade. Water lilies and other aquatics need their fill of sunshine, and while overhanging trees can be most picturesque, falling leaves can foul up the water. In general, a square or circular pool fits in well with a paved patio or lawn, while irregular shapes seem to enhance a rockery.

In designing your pool, arrange for a shelf or shelves because many plants which need only a few inches of water do quite well set on shelves 8 inches wide and deep. When ordering your pool liner, use this easy formula to obtain the right dimensions:

LENGTH = length of pool plus twice maximum depth.

WIDTH = width of pool plus twice maximum depth.

If your pool is 8 feet long and two feet deep, you need a liner that's 12 feet long. If it's 4 feet wide and two feet deep, you need an 8-foot-wide liner.

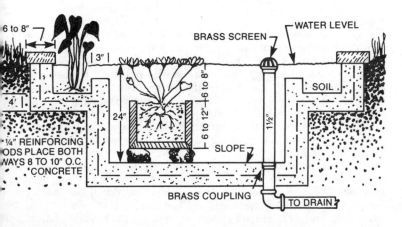

ining the Pool

Although modern pool liners are ugh, a sharp stone can cause amage. So, after digging out the hole, ne the base with some sawdust, peat damp newsprint. Lay the liner over e excavation and pull it fairly taut. old it in position by piling the garden ller, bricks or other heavy objects ong the edges, then fill with water. he liner will stretch and take the ape of the prepared hole. When the ol is full, tuck the overlap beneath rips of lawn or paving stones to ake the edges tidy.

Aquatic plants not only beautify a nd, but play a most important part keeping the water clear and the fish ealthy. Specialist nurserymen can be lied upon to advise suitable aqua- cs, including special collections of pating plants, submerged oxygena- rs, marginal growths and water ies.

May and June are favored planting mes for aquatics which do best in astic water-plant containers, thriv- g in these baskets without crowding ut their neighbors. Another advan- ge—basket-grown plants may be oved around the pool and regrouped will.

Give the plants at least a week to settle down before putting any fish in the pool. The recommended propor- tion of fish to pool area is 6 inches of fish—tail included—to every square foot of surface. This means that my 9- by-9-foot pool—81-square-feet—will accommodate 81 6-inch fish. Fish grow so quickly that the much- cheaper 3-inchers are a good buy— they'll be 6 inches long within a year.

The goldfish is a "natural" for the pool, but there are other varieties like the carp and shubunkin. The some- what rare tench, known in Europe as the "doctor-fish," is worth stocking because his bottom-nibbling habits keep the pool clean.

The pool looks like a picture-book pool the first week after it is stocked with plants and fish. Then things seem to go wrong—the clear water turns grey, brown or pea-green—and you wonder what to do. Don't worry too much; if the pool contains the right aquatics, the condition will correct itself in a few weeks. Don't empty it and refill—the trouble will start all over again, and your fish will not be happy with the change of water.

Don't—whatever you do—don't use any of the chemical pool cleaners available because they can harm your fish. Just be patient and let nature sort things out.

Gulls and other fish-eating birds can be a menace to pool fish in some areas. Gulls are frequent visitors to my garden, so I fixed a rather neat mesh fence around the pool and suspended a nylon net over it. These anti-gull precautions also prevent inquisitive cats from fishing in the pool and your own youngsters from falling into the water.

In a new pool the fish need an occasional feeding during the first summer. They never need food in winter, and once things have settled down they fend for themselves pretty well. Not only will they deal at once with any mosquito eggs laid in the pool, but your fish will even pop up out of the pool to deal with low-flying insects.

With a little common-sense observation and precautions—plus a willingness to work—there's no reason why you shouldn't enjoy your pool in The States just as much as I enjoy mine in England. Here's hoping you do.

---

*MAKING THE TWO-HOUR POOL
—STEP-BY-STEP METHODS—*
1: *Use strings to show where to dig.*
2: *Line the base with peat or sawdust.*
3: *Stretch the liner across the pool.*
4: *Secure the edges and fill with water.*
5: *Tuck the overlap down with stones.*
6: *Lower basket gently into water.*
7: *A place to sit and do nothing.*

Now for the heavy stuff: If you are ready to spend hundreds—or thousands—of dollars and want to establish an honest-to-gosh working farm pond, complete with eatable fish and big enough to swim or boat in, here are two articles on the subject from experts. First read what Edwin Harrington has to say:

There's every chance you can hav pond, whether you live on a few acr or a hundred. The water from a sm stream is sufficient. A fraction of t flow from a large stream or river c be diverted, without depreciation serious reduction in irrigation volum Except in dry country, good gradi and cover-cropping of the loc watershed will provide enough wat to keep a pond filled. Nearby sprin sometimes can be piped, or tapp upon excavating into a valley hillside. Even a well that delivers : gallons or more per minute may used to deliver supplementary wat to a pond.

The banks of a good pond should grassy and trimmed to the wate edge. The surface should be clea rippling where fish have surfaced catch an insect, and moving gently the overflow. It should serve pleasant welcome to the fisherm and swimmer of all ages.

The key to a fine pond is prop initial construction. The first consi eration is water volume and availab ity. Do not attempt to build a seco Lake Mead if you depend upon a sm stream, springs, or runoff. Yo county agent, soil conservation fie man, or a skilled excavator can advi on the practical area to consider. If, the other hand, the supply of water unlimited, you may plan on as large pond as is physically and economica ly practical.

Grading should compromise much as possible with the origin slopes; especially avoid extren drops where erosion can occur arou the banks or on the lower side of t dam. It is not advisable to build a lar pond if you have to create a high a steep artificial earthwork. Convers ly, a good grading plan avoids creati areas of shallow water or gradual descending banks, especially likely occur near the upper end of the pon Banks should be fairly sharp, betwe

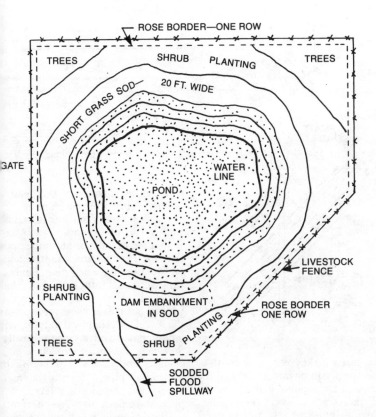

ROSE BORDER—ONE ROW

TREES SHRUB PLANTING TREES

SHORT GRASS SOD 20 FT. WIDE

GATE

WATER LINE

POND

SHRUB PLANTING

DAM EMBANKMENT IN SOD

LIVESTOCK FENCE

ROSE BORDER ONE ROW

TREES SHRUB PLANTING

SODDED FLOOD SPILLWAY

5 and 30 degrees, providing for rapid ropoff to water at least several feet eep to avoid warm and stagnant reas.

Don't go in for fancy curves and ackwaters, since such places slow ater movement, encourage algae rowth and poor oxygenation for fish.

you want an island in the middle, ake sure the banks are fairly steep. he best over-all shape is approxi- ately tear-drop, the upper end ounded off, the deep end at the dam omewhat flattened across the inner urface of the breastwork.

An alternative is the nearly-round ond, where natural grades require a am in the form of a crescent, weeping back a considerable dis- ance along either side to reach higher round. Round ponds are particularly

appropriate if spring fed from below the surface, or if located at the head of a swale that receives surface runoff from a surrounding amphitheater of wooded and sodded areas.

Too many dams have tops that are too narrow. The finished top of any dam should never be less than 15 feet wide, allowing for a 20-degree inside and a 30-degree outside slope. The edges will become rounded in time, reducing top width, and some settling and erosion will take place before a good sod is established and muskrats may start tunneling.

The best control of muskrats is never to let them get started. Fairly steep banks, clean mowing, and no vegetation standing in the water are primary helps in discouraging them. When the pond is shaped, heavy

43

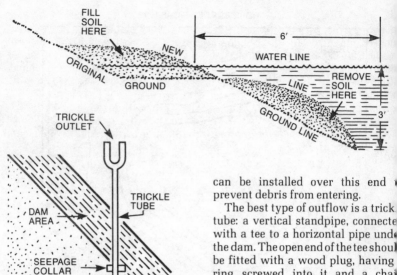

galvanized turkey wire, one-by-two-inch mesh, can be laid all around the banks, from a point just above the anticipated water level to several feet below. A muskrat seldom can overcome this protection. If tunnels are found, it is time to start trapping—in season and according to local law, or with special permission from your game warden.

Where your pond is in a stream valley, the main watercourse should be diverted around the side, in its own channel, or in a newly-created by-pass. At a point slightly above the upper end of the pond, the stream should be slowed and widened by building a loose stone or masonry dam, to form a small pool from which a pipe carries water to the pond. In times of flooding, most of the stream water flows harmlessly through and over the dam; if the force of water reaching the pipe becomes too great, a cover can be temporarily placed over the streamward end. If needed, a screen

can be installed over this end t prevent debris from entering.

The best type of outflow is a trick tube: a vertical standpipe, connecte with a tee to a horizontal pipe und the dam. The open end of the tee shoul be fitted with a wood plug, having ring screwed into it and a cha attached, so that the plug can b yanked out if ever necessary to dra the pond. Mechanical valves, wit long-handled controls, are generally nuisance, becoming rusted fast clogged with debris. In laying th horizontal pipe, concrete or met collars are placed every few feet, t prevent seepage loss. An alternativ outflow, especially in localities wher rainfall is moderate and sudden heav discharge from the pond is not likely t occur, is a slightly depressed are toward one end of the dam, or alon one side near the deep end. Such a overflow point should be kept we sodded, and a few stones scattere about will help break up any rush c water and resultant channeling. Con crete spillways are not generall advisable, since there is a tendency fo water to undermine and cause seriou damage, resulting in a lowering of th pond level.

In some localities, especially wher water volume is limited, the natura soil may not be impervious enough t form a suitable pond bottom. Ther are several solutions to this problem Often, a bed of clay will be expose during excavations which can b ockpiled, then graded over the naped surface of the bottom, and acked into place by the bulldozer reads. Clay can usually be purchased earby, if necessary. In extreme ituations of leakage, bentonite can be urchased and spread over the ottom, either before or after filling, to reate a watertight layer.

As soon as possible after grading, ne banks and surrounding areas hould be raked clean, sown to a uality pasture or utility lawn seed iix, then rolled. From this point of iew, pond construction is best done i early fall to give time for seeding to ike hold. Shrubs or willows can be lanted around the edge—not too lose to the water, to avoid overhang- ig branches or exposed roots. If there s likely to be a water shortage, such voody plants should be omitted.

If you have recently bought a harming "older" property, it may ontain the remnants of a pond. enovation involves the same princi- les previously discussed. Possibly nly a good cleaning, scything and eeding is necessary. But if the banks re in bad shape and water loss is erious, it pays to hire the services of a killed excavator, who will bulldoze way the errors of man and nature and et you off to a proper start. There is no eed to be afraid of a little mud. As the od grows thick and the water ripples rightly, the sloppy mess created by rading will be recalled only in hotographs. A note of caution: aluable trees within reach of the ulldozer's mighty sweep should be rotected with temporary wood uards.

The average pond owner receives a ot of varied advice about fish tocking, fertilizing, weed and algae ontrol. Like so many things in this vorld, moderation is the answer. Pond fertilizing is a major consider- tion, because you want to provide nough nutrients for development of

the tiny single-celled algae that are the basis for plankton. The indirect approach is best; where the acreage of the watershed above the pond is under your control, it can be correctly limed, fertilized and cover-cropped to pros- per and help the pond prosper. A few parts per million of nutrients, dis- solved in water, go a long way toward plankton growth. Runoff water from fertile land can supply the need.

In fertilizing a watershed, a heavy spreading of fresh manure should be avoided, especially near the pond itself. Such spreading can be done just ahead of a plowing and replanting operation, so that the manure is incorporated with the soil and undue amounts are not washed downhill. Manuring is best done in winter and the early spring months so that contamination or serious fouling of the water is ended in time for summer swimming.

Under conditions of poor watershed fertility, where surrounding land is not under your ownership or control, or in rocky and sandy localities, direct treatment of the pond must be undertaken.

Manure may be applied directly to the water with certain precautions. The material should be partially decayed, taken from a heap that has been standing for some time; it should be low in straw content; spreading should avoid the shorelines; and the application should be done in cool weather.

In this way, most of the solids will settle to the deeper bottom, gradually releasing their value; fish and humans will not be greatly offended, and the floating debris will be carried down- stream harmlessly. Organic matter around the edges of a pond bottom, in relatively shallow water, is not wanted. It encourages the growth of sessile algae and grasses, can be stirred up to roil the water, and may create an oxygen shortage that will destroy young fish and tadpoles.

A moderate application of phosphate rock and greensand can be made in early spring, scattered uniformly from a boat or the shore. The average amount would be 250 to 300 pounds of each per surface acre (43,560 square feet), applied every other year. Colloidal phosphate or wood ashes should be avoided. While these are good plant food vehicles, they fail to settle and cause turbid, unhealthy water quality.

Directly liming a pond is seldom worthwhile. Ground limestone is slowly soluble, due to reaction with natural carbon dioxide in the water, and unless judiciously applied is likely to increase the pH of the water to an unwanted alkaline level, discouraging the growth of desirable algae and killing some fish. A spreading of crushed oyster or clam shells can be made, avoiding shallow areas and swimming beaches, to provide a mild alkalizing effect. Surface waters and spring waters of farm and hardwood lands tend to be alkaline, while those of mountainous or pineland areas are usually acid.

The most controversial phase of pond management is weed control. It is unwise to neglect a pond until algae, milfoil, pondweed, duckweed, grasses or cattails take over and then search for some magic treatment. There are situations where the use of copper sulfate or growth regulators may be justified—but reasonable care will solve most of your weed problems. This should include: fairly steep banks plus a constant water level, adequate inflow and outflow to avoid stagnation, well-sodded and mowed banks, no stands of rushes or aquatic growth, stocking the right fish and fishing them hard, maintenance of fertile soil and cover crops on the watershed, and, finally, sufficient fertilizing in the pond itself.

When all of these things are done, the water should have a slight cloudy appearance, caused by the growth desirable single-celled algae, up which insects and small wat creatures feed—the plankton con plex, which in turn provides food f fish. Hence, unwanted growth shou have a rough time getting started. Th combination of plankton and a absence of warm, shallow water spo discourages the development of th large, slimy strands and masses s often seen in a neglected or poorl built pond.

When such algae get starte developing from spores brought in b a water source or by winds, the should be raked or pulled o promptly.

Under no conditions should arsen cal or chlorinated hydrocarbon con pounds be considered for residenti pond treatment. Even in the hands experts, they are dangerous to a vegetation, aquatic life, land animal and humans.

Always Remove Unwanted Weed Growths Immediately

MOST IMPORTANT: whateve unwanted vegetation is destroyed, b any means, it should be removed fro the water as soon as possible an carried away from the watershe Otherwise, spores and seeds may re infest the pond, and decaying materi in the water take up valuable oxyge and cause suffocation of fish.

One of nature's most efficient pon weed controllers is the ordinary duck Domesticated mallards do the bes job, nibbling at weeds and grasse with little damage to bank structur Pekins do a good job, too, but spen more time at the shoreline, pulling ou bits of mud and sod. Two to a doze ducks are the usual limit—the popula tion held to a number that will do thei work without becoming destructive Geese will serve, but they need to b fenced in fairly close to the pond spend less time in the water, and ca be very inhospitable to swimmers o hermen. A simple fowl shelter ould be placed near the shore, or on island (especially if there are dogs foxes roaming the neighborhood), d a daily corn feeding should pplement their foraging.

Ninety-nine swimmers out of a ndred will jump into any water ithout checking bacteriological contions. It is a proper precaution, wever. Many of our streams, rivers d lakes are dangerously contamited by intestinal wastes. Nature has e ability to destroy these organisms adually, as well as many industrial y-products. But when the load is avy, oxygen becomes depleted, ological activity is curtailed, and llution can remain for long disnces.

If your watercourse is questionable, wing through "civilized" areas, it is visable to call upon a commercial boratory or health department to ake biological analyses and advise safety for swimming—a factor that ay govern your decision whether to in for pond building.

Where upstream stretches are genally rural or wooded, there is little anger of serious contamination, nless gross amounts of barnyard astes reach the flow. Normal runoff om the farm lots carries some anure, but natural balance usually xists, so that bacteriological counts ay within reasonable levels. It is ise, however, to fence off the atershed above stream and pond for least several hundred feet to keep razing animals moderately distant. he droppings from a few ducks will ot seriously contaminate the water, nless stagnant conditions exist.

If the water source has satisfactory acteriological qualities, and no polluon occurs in the pond itself, there will ot be any buildup locally. On the ntrary, adequate inflow and outow, proper plankton-insect-fish balnce, and freedom from weeds all assure bacteriological control. And the plankton—that sought-for cloudiness of the water—is quite harmless to swimmers.

Artficial purification of pond water is seldom practical. Most health authorities require a bathing place like a pond, lake or stream to have naturally safe bacteriological qualities, without chemical treatment, or it may not be kept open to the public. There are occasional exceptions when temporary chlorination is warranted, such as after a flood or fish kill; but repeated dosing with chlorine compounds is not going to improve conditions appreciably and can be fatal to valuable fish, both in a captive body of water and downstream.

And now—what about fish? You must decide on the kind of fish that are wanted and suited to the pond, when and where to obtain them, and whether there is a competitive situation existing in the pond already. Old ponds may have a conglomeration of stunted, useless fish, multiplying rapidly but never growing to decent size. They should be eliminated.

The best plan for de-stocking is to drain the pond and leave the fish high and dry to suffocate painlessly. Their remains make good garden fertilizer. If there is any likelihood of causing havoc downstream by allowing mongrel fish to be flushed out in draining, suitable screens should be placed to hold them back—just as there would be a screen at the inflow point to keep out uninvited species.

The most popular fish combination is bass and bluegills, in a ratio of one to ten. Both are good eating and tolerant of differing water qualities. The bass develop mainly by devouring young bluegills, which in turn live on plankton—a complex mixture of small plant, water animal and insect life. The right time to stock is early summer, late enough to be past the main breeding season for bluegills, but allowing a few months for the new fish to become acclimatized. Fingerlings should be one to three inches long, not grown fish.

There are alternative types of stocking. A pond with a fairly generous flow of water, well aerated—as from a hillside or mountain stream—can support a population of trout. Rainbows are best for Western areas, brook trout for the Northeast. But trout may not be stocked with other species. If you are so inclined, the pond can be stocked with catfish. Again, it is useless to try to mix them with other fish.

Most states supply fish from hatcheries, free or at nominal cost. The U.S. Department of the Interior will provide fish to certain users, delivery at the department's convenience; details can be obtained from your extension agent or soil conservation service. There are many commercial hatcheries selling fingerlings in season at moderate cost—either for pickup or shipment.

If you have doubts as to the best kind of fish to stock, whether water temperature and chemical conditions are suitable, and the number of fish to obtain, be sure to contact your local government authority, commerci[al] laboratory consultant, or fish hatc[h]ery representatives. Many factor[s] known to these experts, govern t[he] "carrying capacity" of your pond.

Fishing Pond Rigorously Maintains Natural Balance

Having stocked the pond, there [is] one gospel requirement: FISH! Fi[sh] should be pulled out and eaten, giv[en] away (not sold—that's illegal), ev[en] fed to the house cat. *More ponds a[re] underfished than overfished.* Popul[a]tion crowding results, with ma[ny] small fish, unfit for use, causing a[n] even greater overpopulation. You ca[n] help nature keep the balance, first b[y] stocking properly, then by maintai[n]ing and fertilizing the pond correctl[y], and finally taking that bamboo po[le] down from the wall and using it.

Herons and kingfishers may take[a] fancy to your pond. Do not take alar[m]. At first, it may seem that they a[re] robbing you of good fish. Actuall[y], however, they concentrate on t[he] runts, and more likely are aiding y[ou] against overcrowding. Anyway, n[o] one has ever found a humane metho[d] for chasing them away.

BUILDING A WALL

Stone walls serve many uses—as a permanent boundary line, to give any certain part of your homestead prominence, to level a slope either by raising or lowering it, to build up terraces, to accent curves, to act as a retaining wall for a pond, or become a dam.

There are two types of stone wall—dry and mortared. Both have their advantages and disadvantages. A dry wall, as the name implies, is one in which stones are laid one on top of t[he] other and kept in place by their ow[n] weight. It is the easiest stone wall [to] build and so most of the stone walls [of] the country are dry walls.

A dry wall makes a very goo[d] retaining wall if it is thick enoug[h] because, when built against a bank, i[ts] joints are open and water pressu[re] does not build up. It is more rustic i[n] appearance.

A mortar wall is more permanen[t]

48

Many Italian villa walls of the mortar type are still lovely after 500 years. Such a wall is sturdier, a better choice especially if children or animals are apt to climb and jump over it. In addition, charming effects may be secured in a mortared wall by the use of natural and colored mortars, and more formal effects may be achieved.

The methods of stone selection, laying out and building dry and mortared walls are practically the same, the only difference being in the application of the mortar to hold the stones together.

Before we get to the actual building of the wall, it might be well to point out the relationship between the width and the height so you will not build a top-heavy wall.

For a dry wall 3 feet or less in height, it is not well to build less than two feet thick. For every 6 inches of height beyond 3 feet, increase the width by 4 inches. For a dry wall less than 3 feet high, it is not necessary generally to build a foundation, called by masons a "footing." Careful wall builders suggest, however, that one layer or "course" be laid below the ground level to give the wall more stability. For a wall over 3 feet high, the base should start below the frost line.

Selecting The Stones

There are two big tasks in building a stone wall—getting the stones and laying the wall. Obviously if you have plenty of stones around the place, the temptation is to utilize them no matter if they are suitable or not. In order to build a good wall, however, you must have good stones with flat sides. Six flat sides are, of course, ideal, but you'll find few of these. A stone *should* have a minimum of 3 flat surfaces— one for the outerface, one for the bottom, and one for the top. A certain number of smaller, rounder or irregular stones may be used to fill the interior spaces. This will be made clear later on.

Stones should also be chosen for size, shape and beauty. If possible, choose stones which are longer than they are high. That is, the grain of the stone should, generally, be horizontal. Use flat stones as much as possible and reject round stones, for they give a poor effect and lack stability. To make your wall interesting, select stones in a variety of color. If you can find them, use some covered with moss, which softens the hardness of stone. While it is best to get stones which are either flat or longer than they are high, you should choose a few which are higher than they are wide, so as to give your wall a vertical feeling. Do not place these stones higher than the first or second course, otherwise your wall will look top-heavy. They may also be used to advantage at corners, gates or openings in the wall. But have plenty of long stones and, above all, avoid too many of the same size.

If you can get good stones on your own place, use them. If not, you will have to go afield for them. You may have to do a lot of grubbing and turning over to find the stones you want. In your wanderings, you may run across an old stone wall which the owner will let you remove by choosing stones from it. To a certain extent, this will solve your problem of selection, particularly if the wall is a good one. If there is a stream near your place, you will probably find many flat and interesting stones along its banks or in its bed.

If you haven't available stones and would like to shorten the search, you can buy stones from a number of sources. Any local mason supply outfit will have a stone heap. Most large construction companies have accumulated stone. Quarries may have interesting stones, or a neighboring farmer may have accumulated them in clearing his land.

You can figure the amount of stone you will need by multiplying the length of your wall by its width and then by its height in feet. This gives you the number of cubic feet of stone in the wall. Stone is generally sold by the cubic yard. To get the number of cubic yards of stone which will be needed for your wall, divide the number of cubic feet by 27. Sometimes, though not often, stone is sold by what is called the "perch." A perch is a space of wall approximately 16½ feet long, one foot high and 1½ feet wide—or 24¾ cubic feet. In buying stone, however, you will generally be told to "take all you need" at any price.

Most of the time, the main expense is not in the stone but in transporting it. Stone is heavy stuff and not much of it can be carried at a time except by the biggest trucks, so if you must pay to have it hauled, this can amount to a good figure. If you can use your own car and do your own lifting, you will, of course, save this money. Don't try to carry too many stones at once in your own car as you can damage your springs. Better make more trips or, better still, use a two-wheeled trailer if you have or can get one. And if you're a beginner at laying stone, don't try to accomplish too much at a time. Stone is mighty stubborn and heavy stuff and a sprained back or smashed finger is not pleasant. And a caution—in lifting and carrying stone, carry and hold it as close to your body as possible. Use your arm, not your stomach muscles!

Laying Out The Wall

Your first step in building your stone wall should be to decide on the length, width and height you want it to be. On the location where you plan your wall, outline the total length and width by cord lightly pegged to the ground. Remove any large stumps, bushes and plants or other obstructions within the area thus enclosed.

If the wall is a boundary between your property and your neighbor's, unless he is willing to share the cost and work, make sure that both sides of the wall are on your property. If he shares the wall, then the boundary line should run down the middle.

With the wall thus roughly outlined, begin at one end and drive in a wooden stake at each corner. Masons call these stakes "batter boards" and each stake should be at least 3 to 4 inches higher than the highest point of the wall. Drive them in as nearly vertical or "plumb" as possible.

Now in the same manner, drive in two wooden stakes of the same size and type at the other end of the wall. If the wall is to curve or slope, drive two stakes at each point of turn. Next, tie mason's or other string cord to a stake at one end and run the cord down the outlined wall to the stake at the opposite end, pulling it taut. Do the same on the other side of the wall, so that it is outlined by the cords. With the cord taut, drive stakes at about 8-foot intervals into the ground along the cord, making sure that the cord touches the stakes on their *insides*. The object of these stakes along the cord is to insure that the wall is built straight or with the proper curve if it is not to be a straight wall. The cord has a tendency to sway, especially in a long wall when a wind is blowing.

Now figure what the average height of your first "course" will be by estimating the average height of the largest stones you have accumulated. Loosen the cords on the end stakes and set them two to three inches higher than the average height of the large stones to be used in the first course. Again pull cords taut. Mark on the intervening stakes the point where the cord touches the insides (a small nail may be used). If the cord sags or sways during your work, you can correct it.

Building The Dry Wall

Now you're ready to start building. If you build your wall with a footing, say, of one course under ground level, you'll have to dig a trench in the outlined space. You won't have to worry about matching stones in this trench—just use your flattest and largest stones and lay them as tightly and securely as possible in this shallow trench, trying to make their topsides as nearly level with the ground level as possible.

When your footing is laid, you are ready for the wall itself. The largest stones should be used in the first course. Stones should be laid with their strata or "grain" horizontally, as they are usually found in the fields.

If the starting point does not butt against a house, wall or other object, the corner stones at an open end must have two outer surfaces nearly square as well as flat bottom and top. Beginning at the corner, lay the first stone, making sure its edge is parallel with the cord. Get used to sighting along the cord to make sure the outer edge of each stone is parallel with the cord and does not extend beyond it. Lay one or two such stones along one side, using the same precautions and fitting their sides together as evenly as possible.

Now lay a similar line of two or three stones along the opposite side of the wall, using the same precautions to keep the edges parallel and plumb with the cord. Try to find one or two large stones which you can use to close the end of the wall. You will now have a roughly U-shaped space with stones around the edges and somewhat empty spaces between the outside stones. This space may be filled with smaller stones, known as "backing." They need not be of any special size or shape, but you should try to get as many stones in this space as possible without pushing the outside stones out of place.

Go on placing your first course all along the line. Try to keep your course fairly level. Fill with backing as you build. Large stones placed in the first, or, at most, the second course will give your wall strength and variety. A large stone may be placed in the first course which will extend to the top of the second course; or large flat stones wide enough to extend from one side to the other may be used.

When your first course is built, the second is begun—from either end. Raise your cord two to three inches above the average height of the second course and pull it taut—exactly the same operation as preparing for the first course. As you lay the second course, each stone should bridge the joint below so there will be no continuous vertical joints or "runs." This not only makes a stronger wall, but it looks better. As often as they will work in, "tie" the two sides of the wall together by laying stones whose edges extend from one side of the wall to the other, or lap over lower course stones set in from the opposite side.

To keep the wall plumb or vertical as it increases in height, you can use a level. One end is held against the lower course, the level made vertical, and the stone being placed brought out to touch the level.

(A faster method of keeping the wall parallel and plumb may be used after the beginner has achieved some proficiency. After the "batter boards" have been set out, two cords are run at wall height instead of being set course by course. Small plumb bobs—small stones will do—are tied at 6- to 8-foot intervals along the cords. By sighting along the main cord and a plumb bob line, you can place stones so they'll be both parallel and plumb.)

Keep on laying, filling and "tying in," always making sure that the stones on each course "bridge" the joints of the course below, until your wall has reached the desired height. In a dry wall, what are known as "skimmers" may be placed as the top course. These are broad, flat stones which cannot be easily knocked off by children, dogs and others scrambling over the wall. The top stones are "topping stones"—these are thicker than "skimmers" but not always available. It would do no harm to mortar this top, for performance, even in a dry wall, although this is not essential.

The Mortared Wall

The method of constructing the mortared wall is practically the same as that of the dry wall, the only difference being the application of the mortar to bind the stones together and perhaps to accomplish other architectural effects.

A mortared wall is filled with a mixture of Portland cement, sand and water. Recipes for mortar vary and can be one part of Portland cement to either 2 to 4 parts of sand. A little mason's lime makes the mortar easier to use. Several waterproofing compounds are now available which can be added to the mortar formula. These agents protect the mixture from admitting water or moisture, then freezing and expanding—which can crack the wall and shorten its service life.

Mortar should be well mixed (not soupy) and the color of the mortar may be varied to achieve variety in the outside appearance of the wall. The color may be lightened by using not over 10 per cent of lime putty. It may be darkened by using lampblack. Other colors may be secured from paint supply houses. For a very light-colored wall effect, make an almost flush wall by packing the mortar in the joints and wash the entire surface with a rather thin mixture of white cement and sand. For a still whiter surface, mix white cement with white sand.

Mortar is applied as you build the wall. As each course is finished in exactly the same way as a dry wall, throw some mortar loosely into the crevices which are left after you have placed the filling or small stones between the two outside walls. Do not force the mortar into the crevices, as

you do not want to make a solid wall. Just toss it in. It will settle and harden by itself. When mortar is used, poorer stone may be used for backing.

In a mortar wall, you may sometimes want to give the actual effect of a dry wall. Use mortar in the center and force some of it toward the outside joints from inside (outside application is apt to mess up faces of stone), but do not put any mortar any further out than two to 6 inches from the outside surface of the wall. That is, the mortar should not be visible from the outside. This technique of using mortar on the interior might be used in the dry wall at the ends bordering on a driveway to prevent errant traffic from knocking down your wall.

A charming wall surface may be secured in a mortar wall by coating 50 per cent of the outside surface of the wall with the mortar and leaving half of the stones showing through. Variety can also be secured by varying the color of the mortar, as previously described, and the color of the stone.

Terrace Walls

Terrace walls or walls which are used to level off part of your grounds are actually retaining walls—they retain earth behind them. Retaining walls may either be dry or mortared.

In building a retaining wall one main additional factor must be kept in mind. A retaining wall must have sufficient "batter" or slope. This slope is toward the earth to be retained. When the retained earth freezes, it expands; if the wall were vertical the stones would eventually topple over. By sloping toward the earth, the stones tend to go back into place when the frost leaves the earth. About 4 inches of slope for each two feet of wall height is sufficient.

A dry retaining wall may be constructed without a footing; if given plenty of "batter" the wall will survive the ravages of freezing and thawing.

A mortar wall should have a footing

that extends below the frost line. In addition, it should have drainage holes provided by placing tiles in the lower section of wall at intervals—a small tile about every 8 feet ought to be sufficient.

Upkeep

A well-made dry stone wall needs practically no care once it is built, except perhaps to replace the top stones which may be knocked off from time to time. Where there is quite a space between joints, you may have had to set in smaller stones to fill the space and these may occasionally have to be forced back. Mortared walls sometimes lose some of their outside mortar due to frost, but this may easily be patched by the addition of more mortar.

Vines are often trained over stone walls to soften their hardness. Sometimes, as in a retaining wall, provision is made for plants in especially constructed wall crevices.

STORAGE

There are four basic ways to profitably store foods—hold them in storage, dry, can or freeze them. While certain of these processes merge into each other, this article will concentrate primarily on the first phase: storage. There are a great number of ways to go about creating a storage area, many of them illustrated on the following pages, and a limited listing of foods which can be handled in this manner.

Vegetables

Chard, beets, carrots, turnips and *rutabagas* should be harvested in late November, after 30-degree nights. Root crops of this type can be stored by removing the tops—do not wash them—and placing in an area just above freezing, with 95 percent humidity. They can be packed in cans, boxes or bins, surrounded by straw, or they can be placed in moist sand, or in any of the outdoor storage pits or root cellars shown.

Cabbage and *Chinese cabbage* should be prepared for storage by removing loose outer leaves. If produce is to be wrapped, roots and stem should be removed; otherwise leave these in place. Wrapped cabbages should be stored at a just-above freezing temperature in a cool, damp area in boxes or bins. When stems and roots are left on, any of the outdoor storage ideas which call for damp soil or sand are effective.

Celery is best maintained by pulling the crop. Leave the tops dry—do not wash. The roots should be placed in slightly moist sand or soil, and the plant maintained at 32 to 34 degrees F. To avoid odor contamination, do not store with cabbage or turnips.

Parsnips, salsify, Jerusalem artichokes and often *carrots* can be left in the ground throughout the winter. To make digging easier, cover the rows with about one foot of leaves or straw before the ground has frozen.

Kohlrabi can be stored, after removal of leaves and roots, at 32 to 34 degrees with 95 percent humidity. Root cellars and basement storage rooms are ideal locations.

Beans, soybeans and *peas* should be shelled and dried. To eliminate fumigation, which is practiced by commercial growers in order to kill weevils, simply heat the crop in an oven for 30 minutes to an hour at a

STORAGE CONTAINERS

In most of the storage areas illustrated there is a need for small containers. Below are several suggestions:

Wooden boxes—used for apples and other fruits originally, they make ideal small storage units to be placed in root cellars or larger areas. Interior packing can be leaves (dry and crisp), hay, straw, string-sphagnum moss or crumpled burlap. When stacking boxes, place furring strips between them, the floor and other tiers to permit full air circulation.

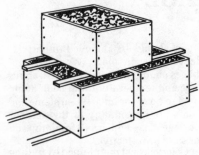

Metal tins—Adaptable for nut storage (see nut section). Also can be used open-topped in place of barrels and boxes. Be certain that rusting is a minimal factor by using galvanized metals, or patch-painting raw metal areas.

Pails, baskets—similar treatment as boxes. Layer packing materials and produce alternately, finishing with two inches or more of packing at the top. Used in pit storage as well as larger units.

Crates (orange) or mesh bags—excellent for onion storage. Remember to keep above freezing. Should onions ever freeze, allow them to thaw naturally before handling.

Bins—Used primarily in larger storage units, these can be constructed some four inches off the floor. Good for potato and other root crops.

Water-tight barrels—pack similarly to pails and baskets. Use as described in storage area illustration.

sustained temperature of 135 degrees. Spread the vegetable in pans for this treatment, and do not let the temperature drop or rise significantly. After drying thoroughly, place in jars or

bags for storage. The temperature of the storage area is not important, but it must be dry.

Onions must be cured. Leave the vegetable on the ground after pulling

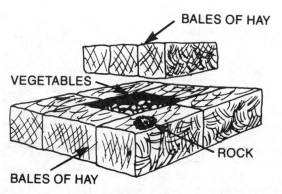

BALES OF HAY

VEGETABLES

BALES OF HAY

ROCK

Top of ground—suitable for most root crops. A rectangle of hay bales, with center partially hay-filled and final bales for a lid. A stone can be placed under the top bales for ventilation, then removed when freezing weather prevails.

for at least two to three days, then place in crates in an open shed for several weeks to complete curing. Remove the tops and store in bins or string bags at temperatures ranging from 33 to 45 degrees with 60 to 75 percent humidity. Attics often prove to be good storage areas.

Pumpkins and *squash* must also be cured. Leave them in the field for two weeks after picking. Leave a partial stem on the fruit, and take exceptional care to prevent bruising, storing only the best undamaged produce. After curing, place them gently on shelves, separated from each other, in a 50 to 60 degree dry place. They should last for five to six months.

Potatoes must be stored in the dark. For several months after harvest they can be held in almost any storage location, as this is their normal resting cycle. After this period, temperatures between 34 and 41 degrees are necessary to prevent sprouting. The lower temperatures tend to turn starch to sugar and sweeten the vegetable. Only experience with the crop will enable you to determine proper storage in your area. During the storage period, moisture should remain high. Never store with apples.

Sweet potatoes should be free from injury, and need to be cured before final storage. One writer suggests the wooden floor of a barn driveway which can be opened at both ends, as an ideal curing site. Lots of air circulation and high temperature over a period of ten days to three weeks is necessary to eliminate excess water, change some starch to sugar, and cause "corking over" of cuts in the skin. After curing, sweet potatoes should be placed in a warm, 50-to-60 degree room which is well ventilated with moderate—up to 75 percent—humidity.

Fruits

Many major fruits do not take storage for extended periods of time. Of the ones that do (principally apples and pears), the varieties vary in keeping quality. The *Winesap* and *Yellow Newton* are among the best apples, frequently lasting from five to eight months satisfactorily. Next in keeping quality are the *Stayman Winesap, Northern Spy, York Imperial, Arkansas Black Twig, Baldwin, Ben Davis* and *Rome Beauty*. Normal storage figures range from four to six months in this grouping. Among those apples which can be stored for shorter periods (two to five months) are the following: *Jonathan, McIntosh, Cortland* and *Delicious* (red or golden). Other factors must be considered:

locality (i.e. *McIntosh* apples grown in New England store better than those grown in the Middle Atlantic States), seasonal conditions, maturity when picked and length of time between picking and storing.

Good keeping qualities are increased with careful handling to prevent bruising. Storage at between 30 degrees to 32 degrees and 85 to 90 percent humidity is preferred for most varities, *Yellow Newton, Rhode Island Greening* and *McIntosh* are better when stored at 36 degrees to 38 degrees. Wrapping with oiled paper or in shredded oiled paper helps prevent scald, acknowledged to be the most serious disorder.

While many of the illustrated storage ideas shown in the vegetable section are suitable for fruit storage, fruit should never be stored with potatoes, turnips or cabbage. The gases released from apples in respiration can sprout potatoes, while cabbage and turnips can transmit their odor to apples and pears. Free air circulation in fruit storage areas is essential to remove volatile gaseous substances released by the produce.

Pears can be held for periods of from two to seven months depending on variety. *Winter Nelis, Anjou* and *Easter Beurre* are the most hardy, with

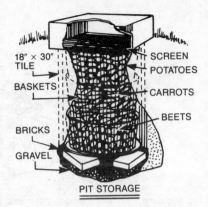

PIT STORAGE

Large (18" x 30", or 24" x 24") tiles can be placed in a pit on well-drained soil. Positioning should be near the kitchen and shaded from sun. As many as 3-4 baskets, boxes or other containers can be held in each pit. A simpler version of the tile pit consists of a 20-gallon garbage pail inserted into a hole. Produce can be placed directly into the pail, but there is some eventual danger of rusting after several years' usage.

Bosc, Kieffer, Bartlett, Comice and *Hardy* in the lower range. Pears should be removed from the tree when dark green coloring begins to lighten and the lenticels have corked over. Ideal storage is around 32 degrees with humidity in the 90 to 95 percent range.

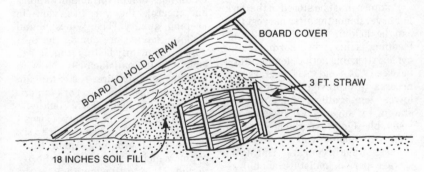

A barrel pit for vegetables or fruit is made by partially burying a barrel with earth and covering with straw and used lumber.

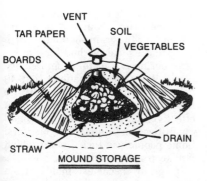

VENT
TAR PAPER
SOIL
VEGETABLES
BOARDS
DRAIN
STRAW

MOUND STORAGE

Mound storage is easily available by placing straw or hay on the ground, placing vegetables on top of it, and covering with more mulch, then soil, then boarding. A ventilating pipe can be included (which should be capped in freezing weather). Drainage must be trenched in around the mound.

Grains

Growing organic grain is a satisfying operation, but improper storage can lose all the advantages inherent in the process. The old-time farmer used to cut and bind grain in sheaves, where it stood and cured gradually in the fields before being threshed. Today's mechanized methods save time, but have certain disadvantages. When grain is harvested by combine, it is cut, hulled and poured into 100 pound bags, but it is still "green" and must be treated with care to prevent mold. It may seem dry, but it will continue to give off moisture for over a month. Furthermore wild garlic, ragweed and other seeds will be included in each bag. The grain must be cleaned with a fan seed cleaner, or winnowed outdoors by throwing it up in a breeze or dropping it past a fan to blow away chaff. Once cleaned, bags should be placed on end on slats in a dry place (not on a dirt or concrete floor), and separated by several inches to allow air circulation. The presence of a good cat will prevent mouse damage—otherwise use a metal, screened enclosure. After a few days, invert the bags and disturb the grain to permit

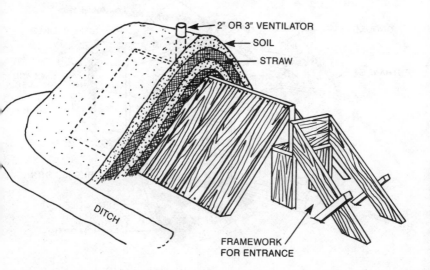

2" OR 3" VENTILATOR
SOIL
STRAW
DITCH
FRAMEWORK FOR ENTRANCE

A box pit (above) is another version which permits removal of small units at a time. Fruits or vegetables are stored in small boxes or baskets (1-2 weeks' supply to a box). Removal as desired.

The old-fashioned root cellar is seldom seen today, and can be adapted from a cave, or built into a bank. Other versions can be seen on the opposite page, including a modern root cellar and one fabricated from an old auto truck body.

air to reach all kernels. Invert again each week for about a month after which time the grain should be cured. The most logical method for storage after curing is a metal drum in a dry place. We have indications that 40 degree temperature with humidity no higher than 50 percent has proven effective for bulk storage. Small quantities can be stored in glass jars. Some people use their freezer which will keep grain indefinitely.

If grain becomes moldy from inadvertent exposure to moisture, it may not be a complete loss. Just wash in plain lukewarm water several times and dry over a hot-air furnace grate or similar source of warmth. You can tell from the smell whether it is still musty or not.

Seeds

Many garden vegetable seeds can be stored for longer periods of time than

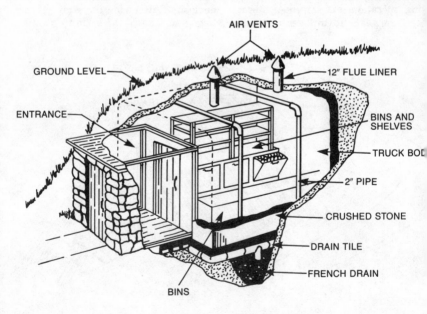

John Keck of the Organic Experimental Farm used this arrangement to convert an old truck body into a storage area. Plan #FS-3 is available for $2.50.

58

might be suspected. We have known instances of squash or pumpkin seed which sprouted after being shelved for as long as three or four years. Certain grains buried with the Egyptian pharaohs thousands of years ago have been planted and they have grown. In general, low seed-moisture is the critical factor. It is important to maintain fairly cool temperatures and low humidity if seed is to be successfully held for long periods of time. Certain seeds, furthermore, adjust poorly to any attempt at storage . . . principally onion and shelled peanut, celery and sweet corn.

Nuts

The difference between prime flavor and bitterness depends largely upon how promptly outer hulls are removed. It is advisable to hull all varieties within a week after gathering. Black walnuts pose problems in that hulls are tough, porous and contain an acrid staining agent. An old-fashioned corn sheller is useful, but some growers spread the nuts on a hard road and drive over them until

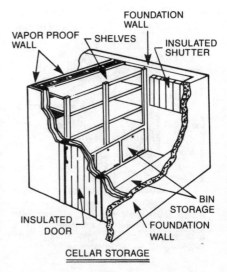

The basement often provides needed space for fruit and vegetable storage, but too much heat and too little humidity frequently cancel out its usefulness. A cellar storage room can be constructed rather easily by the home handyman. Plans for a basement storage area may be secured from Rodale Press (Plan #FS2) for $4.00.

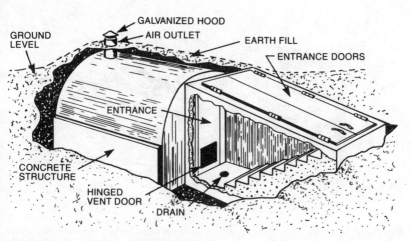

Root cellars such as the above can be built from scratch. Plans including material specifications can be secured by sending $4.00 to Rodale Press, Inc., Emmaus, Penna. 18049. Request plan #FS-1.

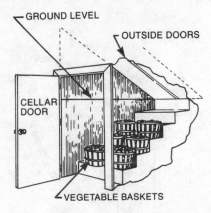

- GROUND LEVEL
- OUTSIDE DOORS
- CELLAR DOOR
- VEGETABLE BASKETS

If your house has a sloping cellar door, with an outside stairwell into the basement, this area can be adapted into storage with relative ease, and little expense.

darkened well-ventilated location is best. Place nuts in wire trays (no more than two layers deep) for periods of two to six weeks until cured. After curing, nuts still in their shells may be stored in attics (for up to a year) but cool underground cellars may be preferable.* It is believed that moderately low temperatures keep the oil in the kernel from turning rancid.

Once a nut has been cracked and the kernel removed, the ordinary kitchen refrigerator is as good a depository as any. Kernels should be placed in tight jars or plastic bags and maintained at a temperature of 40 degrees or less. A deep freeze unit is also satisfactory.

*Storage container: large cellophane bags with ventilation holes punched in them, inserted in tin cans lined with paper and tightly closed except for a small hole below the lid. Store at 34 to 40 degrees and inspect regularly for mold or mildew.

they are mashed. In either case, walnuts still in their inner shell should be washed before curing. After hulling all nuts should be dried gradually by exposure to moving air. A clean, cool,

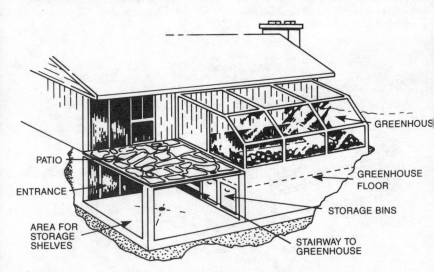

- GREENHOUSE
- PATIO
- GREENHOUSE FLOOR
- ENTRANCE
- STORAGE BINS
- AREA FOR STORAGE SHELVES
- STAIRWAY TO GREENHOUSE

When building a new home, a simple extension of the cellar footings can offer the unique combination of an outer storage area plus a greenhouse. What can be better — winter growing plus winter storage! Plans will be available. Ask for plan #FS-4.

BUILDING WITH CONCRETE

There comes a time in nearly everyone's life when he or she wants to create something that will last "forever"—sort of like a monument. Many homesteaders find the realization of the urge working in concrete. Even if your concrete creation won't last forever, you can bet that it'll be there for a heck of a long time.

On a more practical side, concrete is strong, cheap and extremely versatile.

Our old friend Vollie Tripp has some advice on the general handling of a concrete project:

Every gardener should know how to work with cement. There are literally scores of fixtures to make your garden more productive and attractive, and easier to work. There are walls and walks, curbs and borders, mulch pits, fish ponds, bird baths and compost enclosures. One thing more—cement is the best building buy today because its price has stayed down.

Plan in Advance and—Get Help

If you intend to build a large structure like a wall, or flat work requiring two or more cubic yards of concrete, it will be better to form up your job, and order enough pre-mix, or ready-mix, to fill it. The pre-mix people will deliver a good rich mix anywhere they can get their big trucks, and pour it into your forms. But, someone must be there to see that it is well-tamped and settled, or that flat work is finished off properly. Laying and finishing sidewalks and floors usually calls for more strength and skill than the average amateur has. The answer? Get help.

If you're starting a project, it's a good idea to have a couple of yards—there are 27 cubic feet to the yard—of ordinary river sand on hand. For ordinary purposes, a wheelbarrow makes a good mixing or mortar box. Make sure you wash it out thoroughly when the job is done, as concrete sticks tight to metal, and is hard to get off, once it sets up. The same rule applies to tools used on the job.

Most gardeners already have the necessary tools. A common hoe is just the thing to mix the batch and a shovel will be needed to place it where it goes. An ordinary pointed, or mason's, trowel is needed for doing brick and stonework. For finishing walks, floors and steps, you will need a flat, or plasterer's trowel.

There are several kinds of cement available. Tile setters use a very white variety. Then there is the waterproof kind, while the general all-purpose which comes in 94-pound paper bags does very well for nearly all jobs. Buy cement as you need it because it deteriorates rapidly and once wet, soon is useless.

Making the Mix

For walls and floors, a dry-volume "mix" of one part cement, two parts sand, and 4 parts crushed stone or aggregate makes a satisfactory concrete—providing you have a power mixer. If you do the mixing by hand, forget the aggregate—it's too much hard work.

For general use about the garden and home, I use a mix of one part cement to 4 parts clean sand. But to make it go farther, I toss in a lot of small pebbles. The pebbles should be clean and hard, and when used in a wall or a walk, should be placed in the center of the form, or well below the finished side of the walk, steps or floor. Otherwise they will show when the form is removed.

Always mix up the cement and the sand first. This is especially advisable when the mixing is to be done by hand. When the cement and sand have been thoroughly mixed together, add water, a little at a time, while chopping and stirring. If the sand is dry, it will require more water than when damp. A little experience will tell you how much water to use. The resulting "mud" should be thin enough to fill in the form readily, yet not so thin that the water tends to stand upon the wet mix.

Since chemical action begins as soon as the cement is wet, the batch should be poured as soon as convenient for maximum strength. Although it takes several hours to harden so it will not pour, concrete can lose 25 to 30 percent of its strength through delay.

To get a top-quality job, several things are necessary. One is to have adequate footings, or a foundation for your structure. The footing should extend well into the ground, and be well-compacted by water or tamping. In sections where the frost line goes deep, greater foundation depth may be necessary.

Next, the form or mold must be true, neatly and strongly made. The pressure exerted inside a form for a high wall is considerable, so wall forms of any height must be tied and braced in a very secure manner.

The last requisite is to see that the "mud" is tamped and settled into the form, filling it completely. While it is not easy to avoid air pockets, especially when rocks are used to help fill the form, striking on the sides of the form with a mallet is a good way to avoid these troublesome "holes".

If you intend to lay a walk, steps, flooring or other concrete forms that require a smooth finish, certain problems will arise. When laying the foundation or flooring for a small building, make your footing a full 12 inches deep below ground level. It may need to be even deeper if you are in a hard frost area. Width should not be less than 10 inches and, if a building permit is required, these dimensions may not be acceptable.

The bottom of the footing trench, as well as the earth where the floor is to be poured, should be well-settled by water or tamping. This is especially true where it has been necessary to place a fill beneath the floor. After the forms are true and level, the pouring may begin.

When concrete has been poured flush with the form, tamped and compacted, it is cut off smooth with a straight-edged board. The finish may then be put on by one of two methods. The older way was to screen some dry sand, or use plaster sand, to make a very rich mix for the top layer. As a rule, one part cement to 2 parts sand was used. This rich but thin mud was then spread over the top of the floor, about ¼ inch deep, trued up with a straight piece of lumber, and troweled down until it was hard and firm. If done properly it makes a very nice floor.

The newer way is to tamp down all aggregate and coarse gravel well below the surface with a regular tamper. It is impossible to get a smooth, neat surface if rough gravel and pieces of rock protrude. The top is then further trued up, tamped and cut with straight-edged timber—a job for two persons. Here experience is a big help, but if the builders have ever observed this operation, they can achieve a good finish.

With the top as true and level as it is

possible to get it with a straight-edged board, pure dry cement is then sprinkled liberally over the surface, and the final work of troweling begun. It may be necessary to add a sprinkle of water to the dry cement, on a hot, windy day.

The goal of every good finisher is to trowel out all marks of his finishing tool or trowel. This is not easy, even for the most skilled. Troweling requires very strong wrists. I have had very good results by finishing up with an ordinary wide paint brush. Sprinkle a little water on the surface, then brush lightly, this way and that. If necessary, add a little pure dry cement. You will soon get the hang of it.

By this method, an amateur can get a real smooth but not glossy texture on the surface. In places subject to icing, it is better than a too-slick surface. This system calls for no great wrist power or skill.

In hot, dry weather, keep the surface damp and cool to prevent too rapid drying. Old sacks, straw or hay are good for this purpose, and the forms may be removed the following morning. Concrete will "set" in a few hours, but does not get fully hard and dry for several days. Keep off the finished floor for a few days, or protect it with something. Don't forget the anchor bolts if you're building a structure, and don't lay concrete in very cold weather—freezing may ruin it.

A FOOD DRYER

Out in California, organic fruit grower Elmer A. Kulsar once found himself with a five-acre crop of dead-ripe persimmons. He solved the problem, avoiding spoilage, in this manner:

Using 1-by-2 lumber, I made 4 rectangular frames, 18 inches wide by 24 inches long, nailing them together with thin, cement-coated 6-penny nails. I then tacked cheesecloth over these frames to hold the fruit, while allowing warm air to flow through them. Later, wire screen or hardware cloth could be used to make a more durable tray for future use.

Since we planned to use an old kerosene heater, I cut 4 legs from 2-by-2 stock, each 60 inches long, which allowed me to set the trays about 12 inches above the heater. I next cut two pieces of ¼-inch plywood for the sides, each 24 by 34 inches, and nailed them flush to the legs, 24 inches apart and 2

inches down from the top to allow the warm air to escape.

Then, after cutting 8 24-inch-long strips of 1-by-2 cleating, I nailed them to the sides 6 inches apart above the plywood to hold the trays securely. I made the 22-by-34-inch back out of ¼-inch plywood, and nailed it in place, again leaving a 2-inch gap at the top, and spacing the sides 18½ inches apart so the tray could slide easily. The top, cut 22 by 24 inches, also allowed an 18½-inch space between the sides.

To complete my hastily-made but effective dryer, I added a 22-inch spacer strip to secure the front legs, and hung a 22-by-34 front door on a pair of nails. Finally, I set the heater in position, and hung sheet metal to serve as a heat diverter. We were now ready to begin drying our ripe persimmons.

Most of the material which I had used was not new, but cut from lumber that was secondhand or left over from other jobs. But even if you purchase all new material, here is what you would need:

46 feet of 1-by-2
20 feet of 2-by-2
1 4-by-8 sheet of ¼-inch plywood
3 yards of cheesecloth

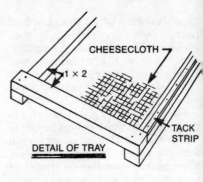

DETAIL OF TRAY

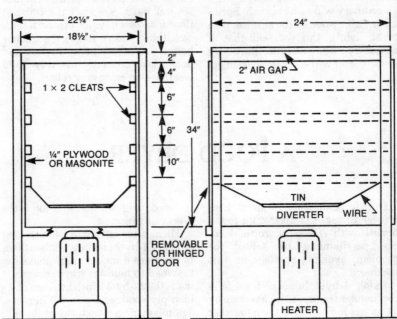

Here we purchase sheets of plywood. However, if you ask for damaged sheets—which every lumberyard invariably has—the cost can be brought down even more.

Any type of heater can be used providing it supplies a steady flow of heat at a moderate and fairly even temperature. An old gas plate, electric hot plate, electric heat lamp or kerosene heater, clean and adjusted so as not to smoke, will dry fruit satisfactorily. Anything that produces a steady flow of warm air circulating upward through the trays of fruit will do the job.

Too much heat is bad, so the distance under the bottom tray will have to be adjusted. Drying time can be cut down, and production stepped up, if the shrinking fruit is periodically moved closer together on the trays and shifted downward from the upper trays. Fresh-cut fruit is then added to the top tray.

To finish my story about the persimmons—they made some of the most tasteful and delicious dried fruit it has ever been my pleasure to eat. You can do equally as well with your own home-grown surplus fruit, and once you do, you will never be without this appetizing and delectable addition to your winter diet.

A RAIL FENCE

The very words "rail fence" probably evoke a mental picture of Abe Lincoln working on his Illinois homestead—at least if you're over 40. But we found a modern rail splitter in John Seginski of Reno, Nv., of all places. John digs the fact that he can sit back and do nothing while his neighbors with painted fences perform the ritual of repainting them. The raw wood of a split-rail fence just gets better looking as it gets older, and with no maintenance required.

The fence is easy to build and calls for only simple tools. While most lumberyards stock the split rails and posts, you can split the wood yourself—if you're hearty enough. I used 4-by-5 inch timber for the posts, and 2-by-4 inch "grape stakes" for the rails. But, depending on the size of your yard, you can work with larger or smaller posts and rails.

Any kind of wood may be used, but redwood, cedar or cypress are more resistant to decay and termites than other woods. Regardless of what kind of wood is used for the posts, the portion that comes in contact with the ground should be treated with linseed oil which can be applied with a brush. Keep the preservative away from the part of the fence that's above ground—it can spoil its appearance.

Lay the posts and rails alongside the actual location where they will be installed. Position the posts so that the rails are longer than necessary. Re-member, these rails are not perfect, and the bends and crooks can subtract from the total end-to-end length. Also, buy your posts longer than needed—they will be cut to proper height after they are set in the ground.

When the posts and rails are laid in place, the post-hole digging begins. Put on your old clothes; prepare to get a little dirty. If the ground is too hard for digging, give it a good water soaking, or use a pick or long bar for breaking the earth.

When the holes are about 18 inches deep, drop the posts in place, brace them, check for plumb, and fill in around them with earth and rocks. For an extra-sturdy fence, concrete can be poured around the posts. I didn't use concrete because of the compact and rocky nature of my soil. If the installed posts are too high, saw them to the desired height. My posts are 42 inches above ground level, and the rail length is 10 feet except where I had to shorten them for better looks.

The rails can now be put into place. On my fence I used a grooved joint or "dado" because of its strength and rustic look. Each rail is different in end size; so every grooved joint was custom-cut for each particular rail. After I cut the one end groove with a handsaw, I held the rail in place and measured the other end. All my rails had to be trimmed to proper length as I went along, and each grooved joint was made secure with two large nails.

If you use redwood as I did, make sure your nails are galvanized, because plain nails corrode very fast in redwood. When joints don't fit perfectly and you have a gap, don't worry—use a piece of the chipped-out, grooved joint to plug the gap. Remember, it's rustic and not supposed to be perfect.

Don't work for a level fence if your yard is hilly. Make all the posts the same height, and ignore the spirit level. A rustic fence looks better following the contours of the land. Finally, when all the rails are installed, clean up the mess, hose the sawdust off the fence—and leave it alone.

You'll never have to touch it again.

AN ARBOR

Most people think only of grapes when arbors are mentioned, but roses, wisteria, gourds, melons and all sorts of things can "use" an arbor.

David A. Caccia of Barnsboro, NJ, has given the subject a lot of thought, and built a successful, basic arbor that you can copy:

Regardless of the size or design of the arbor you choose, it must be built to last. Once your grapevines have grown to maturity, it will be difficult to repair a rotting arbor. For maximum durability, use concrete posts. A wooden form is made to cast the posts in. Making the posts 8 foot long will allow for sinking each one two feet into the ground to provide a 6-foot-high arbor. A 5x5-inch cross-section will give a sturdy post. Be sure to use some reinforcing bars in the concrete. A concrete mixture of one part cement, two parts sand and three parts gravel should be used. The overhead framework can be fabricated from galvanized iron pipe—one-inch pipe for the main frame and a smaller size for the crossbars.

If you prefer a wooden arbor, there are several choices of construction. The simplest is to use cedar posts, with framework of cedar or other durable wood. Use galvanized (hot-dipped) nails to secure. If you use pine, fir or other less durable wood, it should be treated with a wood preservative. Don't use creosote except on the bottom of the posts, or it will injure the vines. Any wood other than red cedar or black locust, if used for posts, should not go into the ground but be supported atop concrete footings that will hold them at least 6 inches off the ground.

If you have the patience, an unusual arbor can be made of espaliered fruit trees. A temporary frame will be needed to train the trees. Of course, no vines would be used on this arbor.

The accompanying sketch shows a cedar pole arbor. Get good sized poles about 6 inches in diameter and 8 feet long. Stripping off the bark will discourage boring insects. Cut a flat at the top end of each pole to receive the 2x8 side-stringers. These in turn are notched to receive the 2x4 crosspieces. The crosspieces can also be notched to give greater rigidity to the frame. With the poles set two feet into the ground, no bracing should be needed. If you wish, 1x2-inch strips can be set one foot apart on top of the crosspieces running the length of the arbor.

Materials for this arbor (which is 15 feet long) include 6 cedar poles, two 15-foot lengths of 2x8-inch, ten 8-foot lengths of 2x4-inch and hardware. One weekend should see this project from start to finish.

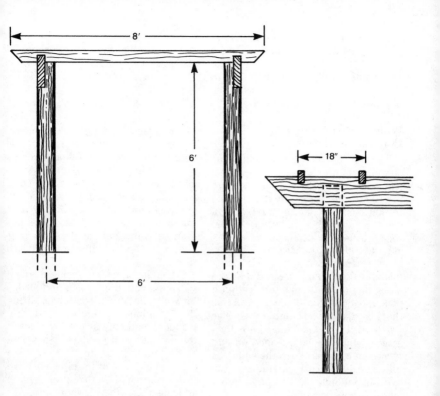

Above: Cedar posts, 6 inches wide by 8 feet long, support the weight of side-stringers and crosspieces. Right: If the poles sit two feet in the earth, no braces will be needed. Cut a flat at the top of each post to take the 2 x 8 side-stringers, notched for the 2 x 4 crosspieces. One-by-two-inch strips can be set one inch apart on top of the crosspieces, running the arbor's length.

DIG YOUR OWN SHALLOW WELL

Dig your own shallow well—13 to 25 feet—and save big money!

I have done this 3 different times on 3 different properties, so there is no reason why you can't. All you have to do is rent a posthole digger and auger from a plumbing supply or hardware dealer and go to work. Assuming that the well will be 20 feet deep, this is what you'll need.

Start off with 3 or 4 lengths of 1¼-inch galvanized pipe, 5 feet long, with couplings and a well point. While it may be cumbersome, one 20-foot-long pipe may be used to reduce chances of breakage and the number of couplings. Be sure to select a site close to an electrical outlet so it will be easy to hook up your pump. And, before you start digging, make sure you know all about the local licensing requirements in your area, and be careful to choose a site free of old foundations, boulders, sewer lines or other obstacles. Try to make it as easy for yourself as possible.

Water Table Follows Contours of the Land

The water table tends to follow the contours of the land, sloping down from the hills to the low spots. There are two basic types of water-bearing formations: 1—sand, or a mixture of sand and gravel; 2—and deeper down, rock interlaced with fissures.

Forget about the second category, because you're going to work with a posthole digger and auger. But before using them, dig down a few feet with pick and shovel until you pass all tree roots and other encumbrances. The posthole digger and auger are then inserted into the soil, leaned on and turned in a circle. When the shovel is full, it is lifted gently so it misses the sides of the hole, and emptied into a wheelbarrow or a pile.

As the hole sinks deeper, the extensions of old pipe that will be supplied with the posthole digger and auger must be coupled securely onto the device. At first, the operation is easy, but by the time you hit wet sand at 13 feet or more, you'll be lifting heavy earth out of the hole, hand over hand at a height that may tower over your garage. Here another pair of hands is called for, and the assistance of a friend or neighbor will save a lot of trouble.

Once you hit really wet sand or a small glimmering puddle of water at 13 to 20 feet, and the sand is too slippery to lift, put the posthole digger and auger aside. It is important to stop digging at this stage; eager homeowners all too often bore down past the water table.

The next step is to drive the 4-foot well point all the way into the water-bearing strata. The well point should have a brass filter screen built inside so that it will be protected by the steel skeleton during driving.

Piping the Well

Couple your well point with your 1¼-inch lengths of pipe, using plenty of good pipe compound so the connections are tight. Otherwise you may lose the well point in the sand. Then lower the piping and well point into the hole, working carefully and gently. If you want to spend the extra money, you can first insert a larger-diameter pipe and use it as a casing, slipping the smaller pipe down through it.

When the pipe is set in place, attach a driving coupling or cap and sledge the well point down 4 feet or so, hitting the coupling squarely. A heavy wooden maul may be used in place of the sledgehammer, but a sledge does a better job. Be sure, however, to use a driving coupling, or the pipe will have to be rethreaded. Also stop driving and begin elsewhere if your well point strikes a rock or solid object.

Next, prime the sunken pipe with water, using the garden hose, and attach a hand pump, priming this in turn. You should have sandy water as soon as the pump is primed, and after a half-hour of pumping, the water will be clear and ready to be tested. If you intend to install a 1/3-h.p. electric pump, make certain that there is about 5 feet of water in the pipe, measuring carefully by lowering a tape measure and weight down the pipe. If there is 5 feet or more of water present, the electric pump will operate efficiently and you can fill in the hole around the pipe.

Where surface water contamination is a problem, especially in low-lying areas with no natural drainage, fill the space between the over-size borehole and pipe with cement grout to a depth of 15 feet, or lay a two-foot square of concrete around the pipe.

Wells Deeper than 25 Feet
Mean More Work and Money

If you haven't reached a steady supply of water, you can go deeper, adding another length of pipe. But it's not advisable to go further than 25 feet unless you're ready to work a lot harder and spend more money on an electric pump powerful enough to handle a deep well adequately.

The practical limit for all shallow-well pumps is a lift of 25 feet. Although water theoretically can be drawn up 34 feet, it is not possible because the pump cannot create a perfect vacuum, and there is friction loss in the suction pipe. The only alternative when no water is reached at about 25 feet is to take up the pipe, and begin the process all over again at another site. Most people generally find water at 13-20 feet, but you may have to dig two or three times before you're successful.

Choosing the Right Pump

What pump you install after you hit water depends on how much money you want to spend. Jet, piston, centrifugal and turbine pumps are all satisfactory. The jet-action pump is popular because it is easy to install, doesn't have to be placed over the well, and is simple in operation. Its only real

disadvantage is that its capacity reduces as the lift increases. As mentioned, there are adequate self-priming, 1/3-h.p. jet-action pumps, complete with 20-gallon tanks for as low as $85 (1969 prices), and there are far more elaborate setups costing many times more. The cost of an electric pump without a storage tank is about $70 (1969 prices). But a pump without a tank is not fully automatic, and must be activated each time it is used. It might be a good idea to buy the pump through a plumbing supply dealer and have him install it, or at least have the benefit of his advice.

Water Should be Tested

The water should be tested, whether you drink it or not, and be sure that all connections are tight to prevent air-leakage. The pump itself should be covered when it rains, and disconnected and stored for the winter unless you decide to build a pump house. The water, generally higher in mineral content, will probably prove more beneficial to garden plants than tap water, and the well will enable you to cut down on your water bill, and give you insurance against any watering restrictions that may be imposed during a drought.

BIRDHOUSES

Whether it's Capistrano, California, or Machias, Maine, spring is the time when the swallows come back to pick up where they left off the previous fall. Almost as soon as flying insects make their appearance, the swallows are there to gulp the pests down by the thousands.

Reportedly able to gobble down twice their weight in insects each day,

tree swallows nevertheless are in short supply, possibly because of the shortage of old trees. These friendly fellows like to nest in old tree cavities—hence the name—but are having trouble in finding enough to go around. But they are quite adaptable, and particularly eager birdhouse tenants who lose no time in taking over any available nesting boxes on fence posts out in the field and pasture.

200 Nesting Boxes—
75 Percent Occupancy

I've enjoyed considerable success—highly encouraging—by setting up more than 200 nesting boxes on fence posts with 75 percent occupancy by tree swallows. Before that, there were no swallows in the area at all.

A nesting box on every sixth post gives each family plenty of elbow-room and feeding territory. Most fence posts are 3 to 6 feet high, which seems to be preferred by these sunlovers—who shy away from boxes that do not get sun at least three-fourths of the day.

The most preferred tree swallow nesting box has a 4½-inch square floor, is 9 inches deep, and has a 1½-inch entrance hole drilled 6 inches up. It is vitally important to leave a ventilation space just below the roof on the front, so the very hot air inside can escape. Drainage holes in the floor are also important when windblown rain gets inside.

The inside front wood should be roughened a bit just below the hole to enable the young to claw into something when climbing up to leave the nest. A few dozen nail pits will be satisfactory.

The box should be constructed so that one side can be opened. The easiest way to do this is to fit the front panel in between the two sides and drive just one nail through each side into the front piece just opposite the entrance hole or higher. The front panel then swings open on these "hinges." A nail tapped in lightly at the bottom will hold this swinging panel shut against the floor piece until it's time to clean the box out.

Old nests should be cleaned out before the new nesting to get rid of the overwintering parasites. This will save many of the young. Frilly things like paint and perches can be ignored.

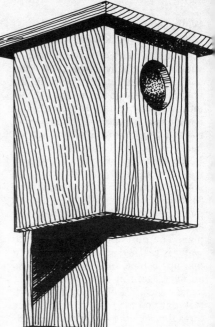

Perches only seem to attract sparrows.

White Feathers Make
An Innerspring Mattress

With the boxes in place, it won't be long before a pair of tree swallows will be carrying pine needles or fine grasses into the boxes, where they'll make a neat bed about 1½ inches deep. Then somewhere—I've never figured out where—they'll find a dozen or so springy white feathers and cap the nest with this "innerspring" mattress. On top of this they'll lay 5 to 7 glossy white eggs, each the size of a man's small fingernail.

For the next two weeks the "DO NOT DISTURB" sign is out while the eggs are being incubated, followed by another two weeks of hectic feeding and rearing activity. During such times when I've gone out to check the nests, I've been dive-bombed by zealous parents not caring who their benefactor was.

In due time though, mama and papa

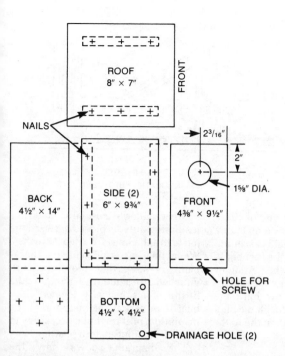

will show off their brood from a nearby wire where they learn the basics in gliding and gulping. In no time they realize that the choicest cuisine can be found hovering over the marshes, meadows and water surfaces. During the summer and early autumn, pre-dusk will find such areas filled with several swallow clans, busy cleaning the air of bothersome insect pests. To watch them is sheer enjoyment.

Many an otherwise silent field lined with idle fence posts can be turned into a haven for the hardpressed tree swallows who'll reward you daily with their aerial daring, and be valuable allies in insect control. Why not give it a try? Put those fence posts to work!

SAVE MONEY ON THIS WINTER'S FUEL BILL

Before the next snow arrives, try answering these questions about your home:

1—Is there any insulation between the joists of the attic floor?

2—Does the door to the attic stairs close with reasonable tightness?

3—Will a pan of water freeze in the attic when the outside temperature falls to 20 degrees F. or below?

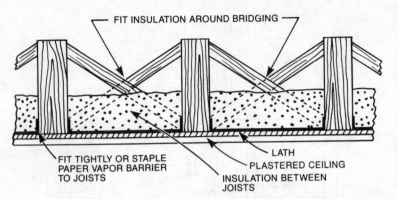

FIT INSULATION AROUND BRIDGING

FIT TIGHTLY OR STAPLE
PAPER VAPOR BARRIER
TO JOISTS

LATH

PLASTERED CEILING

INSULATION BETWEEN
JOISTS

If the answer to just one of these questions is "no," the snow won't tarry for long on your roof, heat is escaping unnecessarily fast, and the fuel bill is larger than it should be. Another consideration, if you stay shivery in the house no matter how hard the furnace works, is that the blame may be not in the furnace, but on the roof.

Here's What Is Wrong

Heat rises. It rises to the ceiling of each floor, and if there is nothing above the ceiling, such as insulation, to stop this upward movement, it goes right through the ceiling to the attic. Then the attic becomes relatively warm and the heat passes through the roof to the outdoors and is lost. If the attic floor is insulated but the stairway door and doorway are not on intimate meeting terms, the heat will soon leak upward around the edges, rise through the attic and depart as before, through the roof.

The attic always will be warmer than outdoors so long as the house below is heated, but for best economy, an open pan of water in the attic should freeze when it is 20 degrees F. outside or a little colder. The water is a good indicator of relative conditions; if it doesn't freeze, too much heat is getting into the attic, somehow.

How to Insulate the Attic

If the attic is unfloored, insulating is easy. Rock wool, glass fiber, or another material specially made for insulating duty, is placed between the joists to a thickness of at least 3 inches. When flooring is present, the placement is somewhat more difficult. Finished attics might even require the lifting of strategically located floor boards to permit the insertion of the insulation, or it might be necessary to blow the insulation into position.

The diagram shows how the insulation fits between the joists. Batts and blankets as they come from the manufacturer will require some cutting, fitting and squeezing. Perlite or vermiculite insulation is granular in form, and may be poured into the space from a bag. In the trade, this is called "fill insulation."

As for the attic door, a soft form of weather stripping will do very well to correct a poor fit. Wind is no factor here, just the natural impulse of warm air to move upward and cold air to move downward, and elaborate caulking isn't needed.

Does Insulating Really Save Money?

As an example of the saving in a small house, one with about 900 square feet of attic, the money value of the heat lost when there is no insulation amounts to approximately 22¢ every 24 hours if the outside temperature doesn't fall below 20 degrees F., even more at lower temperatures. By comparison, 3

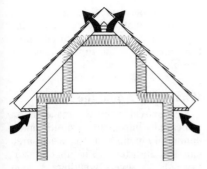

Vented eaves, louvered gables are needed for efficient air wash over insulated ceilings.

inches of insulation reduces the cost to 5¢, a clear saving of around 76¢ out of every dollar chargeable previously against the uninsulated attic.

As a general rule, an attic insulation job pays for itself out of savings in 3 winters or less. And this, as we noted before, isn't all that it does. The heat that is barred from going to the attic stays in the living areas of the house, and makes the provision of comfort that much easier for the furnace. More than once, a furnace that seemed too small became entirely satisfactory after the addition of house insulation.

If You Insulate Your Whole House

The fuel saving if you put insulation in the walls and under the floor, as well as in the attic, is so great that some houses thus insulated can be adequately heated by electric resistance units at reasonable costs. The relative importance of the additional insulation is indicated in the following data on the areas where heat losses occur:

Heat Loss by Areas			
Ceilings	22%	of	the total.
Walls	33%	"	"	"
Floors	1%	"	"	"
Window glass	29%	"	"	"
Leaky Doors and Windows	15%	"	"	"

These data show that, on the average, 56% of all the heat loss which the furnace must make up is through the ceiling, walls and floors, areas subject to improvement by insulation. Weather stripping of the doors and windows, and of course the addition of storm windows, can be counted on to improve the balance.

But complete insulation should be undertaken cautiously. There's a hazard in it too, the hazard of excessive humidity. Cooking, bathing (particularly showers), home laundry, even the breath of the people in the house, contribute water vapor to the air. This moisture has no difficulty in passing through the wallpaper and plaster; thus it gets into the spaces between the wall studding and goes upward through the ceilings into the attic; and if there is enough moisture present, it will condense wherever the colder air can't absorb it. The result can be harmful to the building materials; wood rots and metals rust, and if the insulation is of a kind that absorbs moisture, the development of a sodden mess may follow. There have been occasions when wall insulation has packed down and swelled to such an extent from its intake of moisture that house siding has been exploded outward and required replacement. Obviously, such an insulating job did not pay for itself in the least.

Vapor troubles can happen in a house that has no insulation at all, but generally they don't in frame construction if the studding spaces, the attic, and a basement or crawl space are suitably ventilated. Winter air is notably dry air, and up to a point the vapor that passes through the building materials is readily absorbed and there is no evidence of its presence. In fact, a condition of wintertime throat dryness is quite common, despite the input of moisture from the usual family activities.

When insulation is placed in the walls, the usual ventilation or air movement between the studs is either completely blocked or at least impeded, and the concentration of atmospheric moisture in those spaces increases. With ventilation impractical in most cases, this wall insulation needs the protection of what is called a "vapor barrier," meaning a waterproofed paper, an aluminum roll, or plastic membrane placed on the warm side of the insulation. Unfortunately, such a barrier is limited in its application to either a new house or an existing one whose owner can afford to have the inside walls torn out and replaced after the insulation and barrier are in position.

The alternative treatment for an existing house, and one with which this writer has had considerable success, is to paint the walls with two coats of a rubber emulsion paint. The result is a surface that retards vapor migration quite substantially. Lead and oil paints are reported to be similarly effective, but I have no personal experience with them.

To handle water vapor in the attic, all-year ventilation is recommended. The University of Minnesota Engineering Experiment Station has determined that at least two ventilating openings are essential for all attic spaces. If the space is under a gable or hip roof, ½ square foot of free inlet area and ½ square foot of free outlet area are the minimum requirements for every 300 square feet of attic floor. Thus an attic 40 feet long by 25 feet wide must have a clear inlet of 1.7 square feet approximately, and a clear outlet of the same size.

For an attic under a flat roof, each of the two ventilating openings must be doubled in size; that is, ½ square foot inlet and ½ square foot outlet for every 150 square feet of floor area. If the head room is so restricted that passage through the attic is possible only by creeping, mechanical ventilation by means of a motor-driven fan may become imperative. Such attic spaces should be watched very closely for signs of moisture deterioration, and a fan installed at the first evidence of trouble.

What to Do About the Floor

Floors over a crawl space or an unheated basement (found more commonly in moderate- or warm-area construction) tend to be uncomfortably cold in severe weather. A good way to improve the situation is to add about two inches of insulation under the floor and between the joists. This can be done by nailing chicken wire across the bottom of the joists to support batt or blanket insulation which is on top of the wire and between the joists. Since there will be an air space between the insulation and the floor, there is plenty of room to cover the top of the insulation with a vapor barrier of kraft paper or other suitable vapor-resisting material.

Crawl spaces are substantial moisture producers, since the earth absorbs water vapor when the humidity is high, and rejects it back into the air when the humidity becomes low.

To counteract ground vapor, experts recommend the homeowner provide at least 4 vent openings—one at each corner of the building—and to have them remain open for adequate ventilation all year, even in winter.

Just as a tell-tale, if the windows dump rivulets of water over the sills, or send trickles down to the floor, the humidity in the house is too high. It's time to start the fan in the kitchen if you have one, or else open a kitchen or laundry window a couple of inches and keep it open until the windows dry.

Other Ways to Save on Heating

Don't drop the night temperature in the house more than 5 or 6 degrees. Greater drops will cancel out all the night's saving by making the furnace work extra hard to restore the building to the desired level of comfort.

Another suggestion, if you're cold as a result of all the heat rising to the ceiling, start an electric fan from a position that causes the air movement to go downward. The idea is to mix the high-temperature under-the-ceiling air with the cooler air nearer the floor. The temperature difference between floor and ceiling, especially if the ceiling is a high one, will average 12 to 14 degrees; it may go at times to 20. For ranges such as these, pushing the furnace costs more than is justified by the increase of floor-level comfort; mixing is a better expedient.

And one more thought: don't be afraid to wear enough clothing in the house. In England, inside temperatures of 55 to 60 degrees F. are the rule, and by keeping adequately clad, the reasons for complaint are few.

HOW TO RID THE HOMESTEAD OF RATS

Ever since the days of the Pied Piper mankind has been looking for a quick and easy solution to the rat problem.

But there are no short cuts, and it should be realized that only constant vigilance and good hard work can give us mastery over our ancient enemy, the rat.

Rats are mankind's implacable enemies. They spread animal and human disease, destroy property and have been known to kill wantonly. Each rat eats about 40 pounds of food a year and contaminates perhaps that much more. It is hard to place them on an ecological scale because they seem to be so destructive and uncooperative with other forms of life.

Modern-day rat control is more a matter of applying all known principles than of inventing new techniques. Destroying a few rats here and there in spasmodic campaigns does not begin to solve the problem. Mankind has been doing just that for thousands of years without ridding itself of these persistent and sinister enemies. Any program, to be really and permanently successful, must incorporate these 6 major phases of rat control:

1—General Sanitation
2—Protection of Stored Food
3—Destruction of Rat Homes
4—Ratproofing Buildings
5—Destruction of Rats
6—Community Effort

General Sanitary Practices

Food and shelter are the two most important factors in a rat's existence. It hunts both food and convenient nearby harborage. Eliminate these two attractions and any premises lose their appeal. Ignore them, and new invaders will appear as fast as the old ones are killed off, particularly if nearby areas are undergoing a control program.

Start by completely eliminating open garbage and trash heaps. Avoid spilling food on the ground and leaving it for rats. If birds are being fed, use a ratproof feeding tray, with a generous ledge to prevent spillage. In cities, more food often goes to rats than

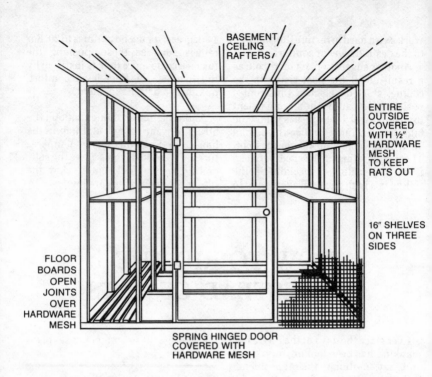

BASEMENT
CEILING
RAFTERS

ENTIRE
OUTSIDE
COVERED
WITH ½"
HARDWARE
MESH
TO KEEP
RATS OUT

16" SHELVES
ON THREE
SIDES

FLOOR
BOARDS
OPEN
JOINTS
OVER
HARDWARE
MESH

SPRING HINGED DOOR
COVERED WITH
HARDWARE MESH

to the birds. Get rid of unsightly dumps, and, if complete burning is not possible, bury debris at least 3 feet deep and compact the earth around it. Let every week be an individual "Clean-up" week.

Protecting Food in Storage

While it is generally conceded that rats can always find enough food to maintain life, you should do everything in your power to make survival as hard as possible. Following this program, a rat baffler is ideal for the storage of foods. As designed by Roy N. Hallowell, the food baffle is a walk-in cage entirely covered by wire mesh on all 6 sides, as shown in the accompanying diagram. Not only does it keep the rats out but, when properly located in an airy part of the cellar, it provides the food with adequate ventilation. A rat baffler about 7 by 9 feet, with the door on one of the seven foot sides, provides ample storage space for a family of 5 or 6. It is a convenient and time-saving place to store and sort supplies.

Destruction of Rat Homes

Unless the places where rats live are destroyed and their potential habitations broken up, control methods are doomed to eventual failure. Rats will continue to survive as long as they have a place to hide where they can rear their young. Studies have shown that, following an intensive poisoning campaign, a rat colony will return to its former size within 9 months or less. Hence, a permanent, complete control program that includes destruction of the rat homes and nests is necessary.

The common brown rat lives underground, beneath stored materials, behind double walls, and other enclosed spaces. These harborages must be eliminated as much as possible. All burrows should be broken up. Stored materials should be placed on racks 12 to 18 inches off the ground. If the woodpile is already stacked for the winter, plan now to build racks for it and place new supplies off the ground. Piles of rubbish and discarded material should never be allowed to accumulate.

If materials are stored in a dirt-floored shed, they should be kept neatly, not piled on the floor. Double walls, made of wall board or other insulating material, are favorite harbors for rats, and should be eliminated. If insulation is needed, nail the insulating board directly to the wall between the studding.

Removal of these breeding spots not only deprives remaining rats of a place to live, but renders the place unattractive to new rats that may stray in.

Making the Buildings Ratproof

A vital part of the rat control program is the ratproofing of all buildings on the homestead after you have destroyed the bulk of the local rat colony. To prevent re-infestation, work with cement, quarter- or half-inch hardware cloth and sheet metal that is 26-gauge or heavier—all good ratproofing materials. Survey carefully the exterior of the building. All openings larger than ½-inch must be closed if rats are to be kept out. Wooden sills and doors at ground level must be sheathed in sheet metal to prevent gnawing. Windows less than 4 feet off the ground, where brown rats are present, and at any height where the climbing rats are prevalent, must be screened with hardware cloth. Foundation walls, particularly where utility lines enter the building, should be checked for openings and pointed up with cement.

When rats are burrowing beneath a foundation to enter a building, install a curtain wall, in the shape of an "L," two feet deep and one foot across the footing. Almost any structure can be made ratproof with a little ingenuity, and at the same time will provide useful and worthwhile repairs to the

building itself. When there are open buildings, such as barns and sheds, make certain that no harborage is present. Then, if a rat does run through the place, he will have no place to hide.

Poisons Are Overrated

"Trying to kill off rats with poison is about as effective as attacking mosquitoes with a blunderbuss," wrote George Milburn in *The Organic Farmer*. His assertion is corroborated by Dr. David E. Davis, Johns Hopkins biologist who states the case thus: "Rapid breeding nullifies any attempt to poison rat populations. Within 6 months after a given number of rats have been killed by poison they have been more than replaced."

Rats start breeding at the age of 3 to 4 months, giving birth to from 4 to 6 litters a year with 6 to 22 young in each litter. U. S. Department of Interior officials estimate that there are two rats for each person in the country and that more rats live on farms than in the city.

E. R. Jennings of the largest exterminating service in the world once said: "Killing off rats by periodical poisoning is a waste of time. It's like taking aspirin for cancer."

The idea that rats could be poisoned effectively was given a boost several years back by the development of Warfarin, a new type of poison that kills by thinning out the blood and slowly weakening the animals. It is much less toxic than red squill, zinc phosphide, sodium fluoroacetate and thallium sulphate—some of the poisons that have been used in the past. We should be thankful for Warfarin to some extent, for those people who want to use rat poison can now do so in greater safety. (Warfarin salesmen have been known to eat some of their product to demonstrate its safety. You have to eat it for a period of several days in order to get the degree of blood thinning necessary to cause death.)

Even Warfarin, though, has its disadvantages. You still have to worry about children or pets who might taste the nice-looking grain over a period of a few days. You still have the problem of poisoned carcasses decomposing and causing odor problems. And unless you destroy the rats' breeding and living spaces, you will find that they come right back.

Trapping is the one certain method that lets you know you've put a rat out of circulation permanently. In 1615 the island of Bermuda suffered from a terrible plague of rats. A law was passed requiring every man on the island to keep 12 traps set. The rats disappeared and there are none in Bermuda today.

The exterminator specialist, E. R. Jennings, has declared that "We refuse to take a job unless the owner or tenant promises to stop up every hole and crack and seal up or eliminate any spaces where rats can nest inside the building."

Trap Where Rats Travel

In trapping, proper placement is far more important than the selection of a bait. Rats follow natural runways as far as possible, along walls and stacked materials, rather than cutting across the middle of the room in the open. Their instinct for stealth and desire for protection causes them to pass behind anything set or leaning against a wall. The best baited trap will rarely entice a rat into the middle of the room. On the other hand, a rat will frequently pass over a trap rather than detour wide into the open.

Despite its reputation, cheese is not an infallible bait. Bacon strips, a piece of fresh fish, or bacon-scented oatmeal is better. Such baits should be tied firmly to the trigger to prevent their being stolen without springing the trap. Do not allow dead rats to decay in the trap. When this happens, scald the trap before re-using, but do not worry about human or rat odors on the trap.

A freshly killed rat in a trap will not frighten other rats away; frequently live rats will feed upon it. Nor is it necessary to throw a trap away once a rat has been caught. If blood or entrails are stuck on the trap, scrape them off before using it again.

The longer a trap is in use, the more likely a rat is to approach it.

Baited traps are not always necessary. Enlarge the trigger surface of an ordinary snap trap with a square of cardboard or a piece of tin, thus making the entire trigger half of the trap a treadle. A square of corrugated paper, with the trigger forced between the two layers of paper, will also serve. If desirable, a smear of bait can be rubbed on the surface.

Traps with the enlarged trigger surfaces should be placed in such a manner as to force the rats to cross over them, blocking a runway behind a box, a beam, or a ledge used as a runway. When laying flat on a surface, straw or shredded paper in a thin layer can be used to make the trap. By using a hose clamp, with a long bolt projection, a trap can be fitted to a pipe by drilling a hole through the trap and fitting it over the projection bolt. A good number of traps is essential for success, and don't expect to catch 5 rats with one trap, but put out considerably more than seems necessary.

Other Methods of Destroying Rats Are Inefficient and Impractical

Many other methods and techniques for killing rats have been advocated, but the 3 general methods discussed here provide the most satisfactory results. Small terrier dogs and, rarely, cats, will kill occasional rats that they find, but cannot rid a premises of the pests. Natural enemies, such as hawks, owls, and snakes, should be encouraged rather than destroyed, but they too, cannot be relied upon to do the whole job.

Virus diseases, supposedly capable of starting an epidemic among rat populations, have attracted some interest, chiefly because of the spectacular nature of the method, but have rarely proved effective. Rats killed by the infected food had to be eaten by another rat to pass on the disease. Also, the bacteria used are known to have caused some human deaths. Some localities have prohibited the sale or use of the so-called rat viruses. For these reasons, they are not recommended.

Other impractical, not recommended methods include adding ground glass to the rat bait and lining the burrows with shards of broken glass. Experience has shown that these methods are not worth the time spent on them.

And Finally, Community Teamwork

The degree of success attained in any rat control program is directly proportional to the extent of participation by the entire community. Every effort should be made to create a continuous, progressive program backed by concerted community effort. It should be obvious that, without the larger effort, individual programs will never attain full and final success.

Education should make it clear that control on a single homestead is next to useless in the long run, if no control is exercised on the next home grounds and the ones next in line. The damage and disease rats spread and wreak on the community should be made known and people whose premises harbor rats should be made aware of the dangers and costs involved. Finally, full use should be made of all available organizations and voluntary groups both for the spreading of information and direct participation.

Nothing less will achieve permanent success in ridding you and your community of rats.

HOW TO USE THE SUN AROUND HOME

How many times have we thought we'd like to put some of the sun's energy to use around the home or homestead, but stopped short at the vision of building rooftop water tanks, piping systems and the like?

It's really not that complicated to use the sun in modest ways, however. And a modest project may give you the confidence to tackle that rooftop heating system some day.

Greenhouses are solar devices, in a way. They admit sunshine during the day, and with enough heat to keep plants from freezing during the night, the gardener can grow things far beyond the normal outdoors growing season. There are several ways to extend the growing season with a greenhouse even without heat provided by fossil fuels.

In the first place, much heat is radiated out of transparent structures during the night. Simply covering—insulating—the structures will maintain some of the heat gathering during the day.

A greenhouse dug into the ground is also more efficient, since it makes use of the heat stored in the earth. Even in northern locations, frost penetrates only a short distance into the earth, and this heat can be used to advantage. Combine this with a simple solar heater which heats water, rocks or air during the day, and releases this heat during the night, and the greenhouse's utility is extended even farther into the winter.

Perhaps the simplest use of solar energy is in the distillation of sea water, or brackish or polluted water. The still consists basically of a trough to hold water, and a transparent cover. The undesirable water evaporates in sunlight, and the water vapor collects on the inside of the cover. As condensation increases, droplets form, and soon they run down the cover to be gathered in receptacles at the sides.

Dr. Farrington Daniels of the Solar Research Laboratory at the University of Wisconsin mentioned an interesting adaptation of this that should be of use to anyone who lives in or travels through desert areas. "No one should ever drive through a desert without a shovel, a clear piece of plastic, and a can or container in the trunk of his car," the solar scientist advises. Then, in case of emergency, it's a simple matter to get water from the earth.

Soil holds water, even if it hasn't rained for a long time. Combining this fact with the principle of solar distillation, you can distill water right out of the earth.

Dig a hole about three feet in diameter and a foot deep. Place the can in the center of the hole, and cover the hole with the clear plastic. Weigh down the edges of the plastic with earth, and place a small stone or weight in the center, over the can.

The sun will "steam" water out of the soil, even if it appears fairly dry. This water vapor will collect on the cover and condense, run down the inverted cone and fall into the can. You won't take a bath, but at least you'll get a drink.

Solar water heating is only a little more complicated, but of much wider practical use. If you've ever left your garden hose out in the sun and come back in late afternoon to find the water hot, you know how the sun can heat water! But this primitive system can be improved on immensely.

Simply covering the hose with a sheet of plastic will increase efficiency. "The air space is very important," Dr. Daniels says.

Solar heaters are feasible from 45 degrees north latitude to 45 degrees south latitude, in areas with more than 2000 hours of sunlight a year. The large amount of heat delivered even on cloudy days is surprising. Tests show you don't need a bright, hot day to heat water.

Of the most commonly used solar water heaters, there are five main types; pan, sinusoidal tube, straight tubes and ducts with heaters, flat plate and Kawai. For more technical material on these devices, see Dr. Daniels' excellent book *Direct Use of the Sun's Energy.*

Space heating of homes and buildings is a little more complicated, but Daniels has devised a simple method for heating homes now used in Pakistan. These homes are only huts, really, they don't have a large area to heat, and the amount of heat needed is minimal. In addition, there is plenty of sunshine available. But the idea could be used in the southern U.S. for barns, greenhouses, vacation homes and similar applications.

Along the south side of the hut, Dr. Daniels excavated a trench that runs under the wall and inside the building. Plastic bags of water are placed in this trench. The water is heated by the sun during the day, and at night the outside portion of the bags is covered to prevent the heat from escaping. The heat is thus radiated inside the hut, since conventional currents are set up in the shallow trenches.

One of the staunchest advocates of space heating with the sun in northern latitudes (and the most experienced) is Harry Thomason, who has built several solar-heated homes in the Washington, D.C., area. There are only 20 solar-heated buildings in the world, so there isn't a great deal of experience in the field.

Many buildings *do* make use of solar energy, of course, with wide expanses of glass on south walls, permitting the sun to enter and warm the furnishings. The use of wide overhangs and deciduous trees provides shade during the summer, when the sun is higher.

Scientists have been trying to get people in several power-poor areas of the world to use solar cookers. They haven't been very successful (which makes some of them look askance at any do-it-yourself projects such as we're discussing here) but the reasons have been more sociological than technical: the women just didn't like cooking outdoors. In America, where outdoor cooking is a treat, this might be something you'd like to experiment with. Since the solar cooker was designed to be built by local people in underdeveloped areas, almost any American handyman can make one.

The Wisconsin solar cooker, developed by Dr. Daniels and his co-workers, is a parabolic mirror constructed with hand tools; of cements, liquid plastics, and one-inch-square mirrors, or aluminized tape. We suspect Mylar would also work. He describes it in his book. Even including the Daniels' book, a survey of the literature on solar energy shows many schemes but few applications. If solar energy is so abundant, requires no transportation, causes no pollution and uses free fuel, what's the hangup? Why isn't everyone using it?

Very simply, we're "tied in" to fossil fuels. When fossil fuels were thought to be in almost endless supply and there were no materials like the cheap plastics we have today for building solar devices, all the research went into developing fossil fuel mechanisms. And today, we're still ignoring the sun and becoming tied into nuclear energy and its horrors.

Even if solar energy were to become economic or necessary overnight, the cost of converting all our machines would be staggering. Gas, oil and coal furnaces, generators, and water heaters wouldn't be replaced without tremendous incentives, because the cost would be in the billions of dollars. Many jobs would be eliminated or changed. Some skills would be obsolete, and others would have to be developed. Solar energy has a long way to go before it can be useful in urban locations, where the area of sunlight per person is not nearly enough to meet current needs.

These are all reasons why scientists believe the first applications will come in areas of the world where there is no cheap power now available, and plenty of sunshine. If solar energy takes hold in these areas, mass production techniques and improved technology might give it a start toward world-wide use.

A RECYCLING SYSTEM FOR SINGLE-FAMILY FARMS AND VILLAGES

In the last few years, considerable attention has been directed to developing a home living unit that offers a maximum of self-sustenance while it is in complete harmony with its external environment. The chief concern is to put minimum burden on both the environment and available resources (especially sources of energy).

The ideal goal is to create a series of "closed" systems in which residues are directly recycled into the individual living unit that generated them.

During our research on the use of algae in the reclaiming of nutrients and water from municipal and agricultural waste waters, and on the development of photosynthetic life-support systems for extraterrestrial applications, we designed a self-contained living system. It consists of an algal regenerative system which has the added advantage of providing for the use of solar energy. Thus it combines addition with preservation, as external solar energy is brought into the system to augment the energy that is conserved within the system.

Bringing in outside energy is essential because no system can operate without a net loss of energy. In our system, solar energy keeps everything running, just as solar energy keeps everything running on earth. Our system has, in miniature, the features of the living part of the earth—photosynthesis for crop production; aerobic and anaerobic bacterial decomposition for the carbon and nitrogen cycles; the recycling of water; plus the use of the chemical energy of methane. This system is beyond the planning stage because its components have been demonstrated in laboratory and pilot-scale studies to be technologically feasible both individually and integrally.

Overall Description

Besides the people and animals, the principal components of the system are: 1—an anaerobic digester; 2—a series of algal growth chambers; 3—a sedimentation chamber: 4—sand beds; 5—a solar still: 6—a gas exchanger.

Because it is combined with a home that requires gas for cooking, the anaerobic digester is covered to allow combustible gas to accumulate under a pressure sufficient to force it from the collector to the stove. Excess gas rich in methane (55-65 percent) is conveyed from the gas dome through conduits into the residence where it is also used for heating. Digested solids are periodically drawn from the digester for use as soil-conditioner or fertilizer in the growth of vegetables on a nearby soil plot.

At its minimum practical size, the algal regenerative system will provide waste disposal and nutrient recycling for four humans, one cow and 50 chickens. This size is arbitrarily

82

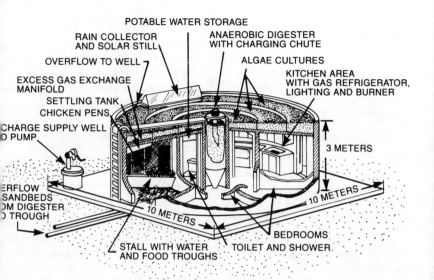

POTABLE WATER STORAGE

RAIN COLLECTOR
AND SOLAR STILL

ANAEROBIC DIGESTER
WITH CHARGING CHUTE

OVERFLOW TO WELL

ALGAE CULTURES

EXCESS GAS EXCHANGE
MANIFOLD

KITCHEN AREA
WITH GAS REFRIGERATOR,
LIGHTING AND BURNER

SETTLING TANK
CHICKEN PENS

CHARGE SUPPLY WELL
D PUMP

3 METERS

ERFLOW
SANDBEDS
M DIGESTER
TROUGH

10 METERS

10 METERS

BEDROOMS

STALL WITH WATER
AND FOOD TROUGHS

TOILET AND SHOWER

Figure 2. Schematic diagram of a dwelling unit for a family of 4 and their livestock which incorporates a microbiological recycle system for water, nutrients, and energy in a convenient and hygienic environment.

considered as the most elementary that is operable. The bases upon which the size of the components of this single-family unit were estimated are described subsequently. But within certain size limits (as yet to be determined), design data proven satisfactory for the single-family unit can be directly expanded to fit larger populations.

The Integrated System

A diagrammatic sketch of a typical family unit of the dimensions given is presented in Figure 2. The operation of the system involves the charging of all manure, urine, wasted food, night soil and clean-up water into the digester shortly after they are produced, or at least once a day. In the digester, fermentation once established continues on a steady basis, as does gas production.

Special care will have to be exercised to avoid unnecessary loss of useful components. Therefore, all solids, liquids and gases must be recycled or consumed. Complex substances are decomposed in the digester. Products of this decomposition are organic acids, ammonia, CO_2 and methane. The methane is stored for use as needed; under slight pressure, it is used for cooking.

The addition of the nutrients to the digester displaces soluble substances into the algal culture, where the latter serve as a base for algal growth. Carbon dioxide, formed by the combustion of the methane, is vented by convection to the algal culture, where a part of it is used as a carbon source by the growing algae.

Algal slurry fed to the cow constitutes its sole source of drinking water, which forces it to consume algal protein in wet form. Algal slurry not consumed by the cow is removed from the trough, and spread over the sand beds. The dewatered and dried algae can be used on the site for chicken feed, also to augment the algal slurry feed for the cow, or sold.

Using the space below the circular algal culture tanks as living quarters gives shelter to both the animals and humans. The algal culture and digester provide a buffer against rapid temperature changes, while the metabolic heat given off by the occupants supplies some warmth to the algal culture and digester during cool periods.

On the basis of past experience, the system can be expected to provide an ample and hygienic environment for a family and its essential livestock. The unit can be constructed of local materials, or perhaps can be prefabricated for import. Because it is largely powered by sunlight energy, the feasibility of such a system is greatest in tropical regions of the world, although it can be of use in other areas during the summer period.

The advantages of the system we have described here are:

1—the creation of a highly livable system for the occupants;
2—the establishment of an efficient and hygienic waste management;
3—the recovery of valuable nutrients from wastes.

A preliminary economic analysis indicates that a gross income of between $250 and $1,000 a year could be realized by operating the system. Operation costs should range from $50 to $100 a year. If only the lower income level ($250) were attained, a substantial subsidy would probably be required. On the other hand, if the higher ($1,000) income level is achieved, the unit probably would be economically attractive.

BUILD A MINIBARN

A garage full of garden tools can give the family car a bad case of rusty nuts and bolts. Or is it the other way with you—the car's inside where it belongs, but the garden tools are all covered with rust?

In either case, it's time to think of building a toolshed which can pay for itself by protecting your tools and power equipment and keeping them in good working order. We built a 7-by-7 shed, about 8 feet high, with a roof that slopes from the front to rear and with a cinder block base and wooden top structure. We have found this small building a useful working addition to the homestead—it provides our two goats with a snug home.

Choose Durable Materials

We chose durable materials because we will always be using our minibarn. I don't recommend hastily scraped-up farm buildings which cost little, but soon fall apart and are a poor investment in the long run.

So we decided on a 4-foot-high cinder block foundation which keeps the wood well off the ground, safe from dampness and termites. The frame is made of 2-by-6's and 2-by-4's with a half-inch plywood exterior roof, covered with asphalt shingles left over from the house. The sides are also leftover—cedar siding used both vertically and horizontally.

Up front we have a door flanked by a pair of windows—glassless because of the goats. Instead, we stapled window screening over the openings, and then covered everything with a half-inch wire mesh. In cold weather we latch plywood panels over the openings. We would have used glass if we were making a toolshed. The overall size was determined by construction convenience—two 4-by-8 plywood sheets form the roof and give us plenty of headroom.

The first step is to lay out the footings. Level the ground, and then drive in 8 stakes for your guidelines as shown in the diagram. Dig a ditch 8 inches deep and wide around the 4 sides. Next mix concrete—one part cement, 3 dry sand, and 5 gravel. Mix it dry and add just enough water so the concrete forms a level surface in the ditch when agitated without being soupy. Fill the ditch 4 to 6 inches, which probably is not below the frost line, so add a few reinforcing bars or iron pipes to the footing.

Working with Cinder Blocks

When the concrete has set, you are ready to lay the cinder blocks. Here are a few basic pointers which have saved me a lot of time and trouble: First, build up the 4 corners. Use a level and be sure each block is level and square. The amount of water you add to the mortar mix is very important. If it is too dry, it will not squeeze out as you tap the block into position. If it is too wet, the weight of the block will squeeze out more than you want. To get a good bond between the mortar and blocks, the blocks should be slightly damp. *Don't work when the mortar might freeze.* Imbed anchor bolts in the mortar as the top row of blocks is laid to hold the 2-by-4 sill in place, so the wooden frame will in turn be secure to the sill.

The 5 roof rafters are 2-by-6's supported at each end by a vertical 2-by-4 which is toenailed to the sill. The roof is simply two sheets of half-inch plywood laid across the rafters. The most economical plywood to use is C-D sheathing with exterior glue. Asphalt shingles are nailed down over the plywood.

To close the sides in, I used some rough cedar boards and ran them vertically from the sill to the roof rafters. A few lengths of leftover horizontal siding closed the rear.

Making the Door

The door consists of one 2-by-8—a 2-by-6 will do—on the hinge side, and a 2-by-4 on the latch side, tied together on the top, bottom and in the middle by 3 horizontal 2-by-4's. I used a lap joint at the 4 corners, then glued and nailed them together. The bottom half of the door is covered with quarter-inch exterior plywood, while the top is covered with window screening. Two heavyweight garage-door hinges give it ample support and ease in handling, while a simple bolt keeps it shut. If you want to be fancy, a padlock will give you extra security, and a coat of white paint will give you a bright interior.

You can save even more if you've got scrap metal and wood stored up on your place. How long the job will take is strictly up to you. About a month of spare time saw mine completed—start to finish.

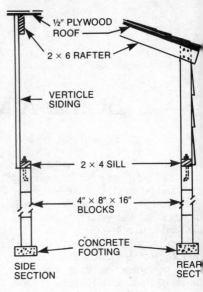

The 4-foot-high cinder block foun-dation means a damp-free structure. Start by building up the corners, and make sure that each block sits level. Above: Profile of barn shows construction details. Note how wooden walls are secured to blocks with anchor bolts, while the roof is two plywood sheets over which asphalt shingles are nailed. The solid and hefty wooden frame consists of 2 x 4 vertical supports and 2 x 6 rafters. Magnification of corner shows jointing of rafters and supports.

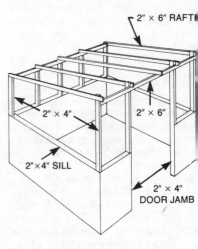

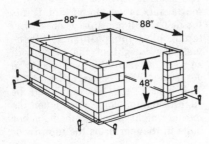

NOTES

NOTES

NOTES

NOTES

NOTES

NOTES

NOTES

NOTES

NOTES

NOTES